SHAUN MOREY
INCREDIBLE
—and true!—
FISHING STORIES

Workman Publishing · New York

P9-DHD-576

Copyright © 2014 by Shaun Morey

All rights reserved. No portion of this book may be reproduced—
mechanically, electronically, or by any other means, including
photocopying—without written permission of the publisher.

Library of Congress Cataloging-in-Publication Data is available.

ISBN 978-0-7611-8017-3

Design by Becky Terhune
Illustrations by Adam Turnbull
Complete photo credits appear on page 212.

Workman books are available at special discounts when purchased in
bulk for premiums and sales promotions as well as for fund-raising or
educational use. Special editions or book excerpts can also be created to
specification. For details, contact the Special Sales Director at the address
below, or send an email to specialmarkets@workman.com.

WORKMAN is a registered trademark of Workman Publishing Co., Inc.

Workman Publishing Company, Inc.
225 Varick Street
New York, NY 10014-4381
workman.com

Printed in the United States of America on responsibly sourced paper.

First printing April 2014

10 9 8 7 6

FOR CONNOR

CONTENTS

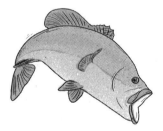

ACKNOWLEDGMENTS

A book like this takes a boatload of cooperation. My sincerest appreciation goes to the anglers and captains whose stories appear in these pages. Your experiences are one of a kind, and many of your catches will be inspirations for generations of anglers to come. For those who helped track down an elusive angler or a busy captain, I thank you.

A special shout-out to good friend and radio host Pete Gray of *Let's Talk Hookup*, to former IGFA president and world-class fisherman Michael Leech, to Randy Ramsey of Jarrett Bay Boatworks, to Steve Morghan of Australia's *Fishing Monthly*, to Michael Neil at the Daytona Boat Dock, to Doug McFetters, to Winston Warr III, and to all the anglers who have sent me letters and emails filled with stories that, while not all in these pages, are certainly worthy of the title "incredible."

And none of this would be possible without a world-class captain and crew. An ocean of gratitude to editor-in-chief Suzie Bolotin, editor Mary Ellen O'Neill, and literary agent Richard Pine. And an especially deep thanks to Peter Workman, in memoriam. These four are among the most professional, dedicated, and creative individuals I know. My debt to you is fathomless.

And to Amanda and Maggie, who join me on the water every chance they get. The fishing is always better with the two of you on board.

PREFACE

Fishing is the only sport I know that offers the trifecta of excitement, adventure, and mystery. It's there in the anticipation of the hunt and the thrilling notion of raising an unknown lunker from the depths. Then there's the possibility of spotting a bald eagle perched atop a riverside pine, or seeing an osprey snatch a trout from the surface of a lake, or hearing a bear crash though the nearby underbrush. There's the exhilaration of seeing a finback whale breaching the ocean's surface after endless hours of trolling, the sudden appearance of seabirds dive-bombing a school of frenzied tuna, the heart-skipping shock of a dorsal fin slicing through a tabletop sea. I have been fishing since the age of two, and still I get butterflies on my way to the dock. I still meet the kindest people, generous and interesting, and all with a story to tell.

In my worldwide search for incredible fishing stories, I have come across reports that stretch the credulity of even the most seasoned storytellers. In this book, the stories identified as "Fishing for the Truth" are ones that were sent to me by readers or that I heard about in my travels. I have attempted to find witnesses to confirm these reports, but have yet to succeed. I do, however, believe these stories to be true, and welcome your comments and corroboration. Please contact me through my website, shaunmorey.com, and I will update the stories online with further information and/or photographs. While at the website, you can view extraordinary photographs, like the thumb found in the belly of the trout; read additional stories; and see videos like the killer bees that scared the bass fishermen out of their boat—literally. I'd also like to hear about your most incredible fishing story. You can post your stories and incredible fishing photos on the website.

While the intentions of this book are to entertain and enthrall, I also hope it serves as a historical snapshot of the extraordinary sport of fishing. I have been surprised again and again at what can happen when the hook hits the water, and I don't want anyone to be deprived of those joys, so please do what you can to sustain our fisheries. Our waters are increasingly under pressure to absorb pollutants and still produce edible fish. And while many rivers and lakes are cleaner today than they were a few decades ago, much more needs to be done. Yes, commercial-fishing quotas have lessened pressure on some of our most vulnerable seagoing species, but still we can do more. Anglers are more cautious about the gear they use, the fishing line they discard, and the fish they place in the cooler. Dams have been removed, allowing wild fish back to their spawning grounds. Still, we must take it upon ourselves to support local causes to better our watersheds and protect our sport.

One of the best ways to help is to take a kid fishing. Recreational anglers have a powerful voice when we are generations strong. Tens of millions of us strive for the same thing: schools of large healthy fish—for ourselves, and our children. So join your local fishing club or angling organization. Volunteer at a kids' fishing derby. Donate time or gear or money to one of the many take-a-kid-fishing foundations. All can be found by a simple Internet search. The more kids we get to the lake or stream or out on a half-day boat, the better our chances of healthy waters and world-record fish. Thank you for anything you can do to help.

Tight lines and singing reels,
Shaun

The author, age 2, fishing with a homemade cane pole.

EPIC BATTLES AND OBSESSIONS

A FULL-BELLIED BATTLE

This 1,805-pound Pacific blue marlin was hooked by Captain Cornelius Choy and those aboard his now-famous charter boat, the *Coreene-C*, off Oahu, Hawaii, on June 10, 1971. The fish was so powerful that it required the additional brawn of three men from Huntington Beach, California, to land the behemoth, thereby disqualifying the catch from a world record. Remarkably, the blue marlin never sounded even though it was hooked in the jaw by a standard lure, and then took only 45 minutes to land. The reason for the short fight may have been the 100-pound yellowfin tuna found partially digested in the marlin's gullet, possibly making it too full to battle the anglers.

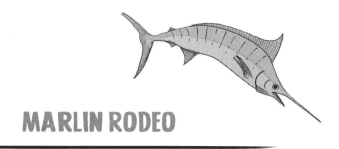

MARLIN RODEO

As host of New Zealand's popular TV series *The Ultimate Fishing Show*, Matt Watson has caught giant bluefin tuna and great white sharks using only a hand line. He crewed on New Zealand's most successful sportfishing boat 4 years in a row, tallying the most marlin caught in a single season. He's caught marlin from a surfboard, and another from a Jet Ski. He's hooked nearly every game fish imaginable, including an enormous swordfish from a hand line, only to have it ravaged by a huge mako shark.

But among the coolest things he's ever done was to leap from a helicopter onto the back of a billfish.

"The idea started while filming in Vanuatu, in the South Pacific," Watson said. "We were heading out to do some land-based fishing on a remote island and we were flying in by helicopter. The pilot was telling me about the cowboys back in New Zealand that would leap from his helicopter to live-capture wild deer during a time when venison meat was at a premium. He'd hover overhead and the cowboys would jump out and wrestle the deer to the ground. It got me to thinking about jumping into the ocean and wrestling a game fish."

Later that evening, the idea of helicopter fishing came up again. Watson's first thought was to try it with a shark. "There were lots of sharks in the bay at that time," he said. "Unfortunately the sharks were spooked by the sound and vibrations of the chopper. Every time we got into position, they would swim deeper."

Eleven months later, Matt was on the northern coast of New Zealand, ready to try again. "The first time I jumped, I landed on a marlin, and got it by the tail. The fish dragged me straight down. We had a cameraman in the water, so I held on hoping for some good footage. I went too deep and didn't realize how heavy my clothes would be. I couldn't make any headway to the surface, but luckily the cameraman was wearing fins and was able to push me to the surface. It was pretty frustrating to come so close and not get the footage.

"I wasn't planning to jump again," Watson said. "But as we were headed back, we came across a dozen or so marlin feeding. The

Watson on the back of a 250-pound marlin

late afternoon sunlight was just right for a shot, so the cameraman got into position, and I removed my shoes and jumped."

FISH FACT

Some fish—like carp minnows and suckers—have teeth in their throats. Other fish have teeth on their tongues and on the roofs of their mouths. The sea lamprey has a toothy tongue that it uses to drill a hole in the body of live fish so that it can suck out blood and bodily fluids.

This time, Watson landed squarely on the marlin's back, stunning the fish. Billfish are top-of-the-food-chain predators and are unaccustomed to attack from above. The game fish froze and the cameraman filmed a first in fishing history. Since then, Watson's resume has grown to include writing for fishing publications, crewing on many of New Zealand's top sportfishing boats, catching and releasing hundreds of big game fish, setting records, assisting with billfish research, and advocating and working for marine conservation groups, including starting his own project to reduce fish waste and feed the needy by utilizing the whole fish.

"I have so many ideas," he explained from his New Zealand office, "that I just hope the show keeps growing so I can try them all."

And what's next for this extraordinary angler? Mexico for starters.

"We're heading to Puerto Vallarta," Watson said excitedly. "I've never caught a roosterfish."

Chances are he will land one of the brutes, and certainly in a way never tried before.

The video of this spectacular marlin ride and many more catches can be seen at ultimatefishing.tv. For Watson's conservation project, go to freefishheads.co.nz.

 # MONSTROUS HALIBUT

It was a pleasant summer day in Tutka Bay, Alaska, 15 miles across from Kachemak Bay near the city of Homer. Glenda Rosenbalm and her husband, Bill, loaded their 18-foot fishing boat for a short but leisurely fishing tour around the bay. Along for the tour were Bill's relatives Ed and Kathy Hodgson.

Glenda, who planned to return within the hour, left a chicken cooking in the oven. Neither she nor Bill brought along a gun, something they always did when halibut fishing. Guns were often used on halibut to end what could become a boated fish flapping its powerful, heavy wings across the deck, crushing gear and bones with abandon.

"We were just excited to get on the water," Glenda recalled. "Kathy and Ed were anxious to see the bay, and we weren't going out for long. The fishing was just a last-minute thought."

Once on the bay, Bill stopped the boat and set the anchor. The fishing lines were baited and lowered to the sandy floor 70 feet below. When 30 minutes passed without a strike, the group decided to head back for supper. Glenda picked up her 6-foot fishing rod strung with 80-pound line and pulled back. The rod bowed forward and the line didn't move.

"I thought I was snagged," Glenda said. "I was trying to decide what to do when I felt a funny movement on the pole. I pulled again, but still nothing happened. It was just like pulling on the side of a barn."

As she turned to ask Bill for help, the line moved. She held the rod steady, felt another movement, and heaved back.

"I knew then that I wasn't snagged," Glenda continued, "because I felt movement. It wasn't much, but it was enough to keep me interested."

The hooked halibut hardly moved, and at 6:30 that evening Glenda was still pulling. She had managed to raise the fish one time, but only briefly and only about 3 feet from the bottom. The halibut hovered for an instant, then settled back into its hole. Bill never had to raise the anchor to follow the fish—it just wasn't moving.

Some commercial boats were anchored nearby, awaiting the following day's opening of salmon season. Soon aware of Glenda's predicament, they called her by radio to offer assistance and support.

"I remember one of the fellas on a commercial boat asking about a gun. When we told him ours was at home, he brought over a little twenty-two-caliber rifle. An hour later, he came back with a thirty-thirty."

The fish still hadn't moved and Glenda was exhausted. Reluctantly she passed the rod to Ed, who beamed with confidence. He accepted the rod and pulled with all his strength, to no avail.

Ed persisted, and during the next hour and a half the fish surfaced once and then settled back into its hole. It was a big fish, the largest halibut they had ever seen.

Glenda Rosenbalm and her estimated 450-pound state record halibut

The Alaskan sky turned to an eerie dusk. Ed worked diligently, but as the hours passed, the mood on board turned to frustration. Glenda, who felt responsible for the catch, announced a new and desperate strategy. She told Ed to tighten the drag and crank in the line. The fish could do what it wanted.

"It was a funny thing," Glenda said. "That great big halibut came straight up without a fight. She must have been really tired. She got to the surface of the water and just laid there."

Ed held the line steady while the commercial fisherman with the .30-.30

took aim and ended the fight. The halibut was towed and then hoisted from the rigging of a nearby commercial boat. Glenda watched in disbelief. The halibut that began as a snag measured almost 8 feet from nose to tail. It was 4 feet wide and 1½ feet thick.

FISH FACT
Cold-water fish have a special type of blood antifreeze that keeps them from dying in icy water.

After some well-deserved victory beers aboard the commercial boat, Bill tied the fish to their small boat and the weary crew returned home. It was well after midnight when they arrived. The chicken dinner was more than cooked, but nobody minded.

The next morning, it took Glenda and Ed 7 hours to butcher the monster halibut. They carved more than 200 pounds of fillets and roasts from the body of the fish. Each cheek, considered a delicacy, weighed a pound and a half.

Glenda removed the 50-pound halibut head and took it to the local Department of Fish and Game. The otolith bone was removed from the fish's ear and sent to the Seattle Halibut Commission for tests. The results concluded that the halibut was a female, age 30.

The Department of Fish and Game used the halibut's measurements to calculate a weight of 450 pounds. If it had been caught within the International Game Fish Association's guidelines—by a single angler—the fish would have set a world record.

"We never thought about world records during the fight," Glenda said. "If I knew how big she was going to be, I never would have given up the rod!"

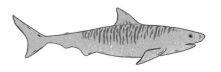

TIGERS ON THE BEACH

Billy Sandifer fishes for sharks. Big sharks. Not from the helm of a high-priced fishing boat or the rusted transom of some commercial longliner. Not surprisingly, Sandifer prefers sand-fishing, specifically along the 60-mile-long barren expanse of South Padre Island, Texas. It's where the tigers come to feast, and it's where Sandifer waits atop his 4-wheel-drive Chevy Suburban, with his inflatable dinghy, heavy fishing gear, and sixth sense for hungry predators.

He first came here after spending time in Vietnam. He set up camp on a lonely stretch of Texas beach, an empty wasteland of sand. For 18 months, Sandifer wandered the shoreline fishing and fighting off memories of the war. The calm, blue water soothed his demons while the sharks fed his need to fight an enemy.

"I learned about the tides, the currents, and the wind. I learned about the sharks and how to catch them. After a year and a half, I guess I knew most everything there was to know out there."

Sandifer, who had become a walking textbook on shark fishing from the surf, finally returned to nearby Corpus Christi and began a business guiding anglers to world-class surf fishing. His specialty? Huge tiger sharks from the beach.

"Back then, when I started out, we killed the sharks we caught. We used the heaviest gear available, three to five hooks buried inside a thirty-, forty-, even sixty-pound bait anchored out in the current with twenty-five pounds of lead. My customers had never experienced anything like it. The exhilaration and sheer exhaustion of fighting five hundred pounds of shark from the beach was a once-in-a-lifetime experience."

Sandifer, now in his sixties, has caught hundreds of the big fins since landing on that empty coastline more than four decades ago. He long ago quit killing the sharks, and instead stands in the shallows and plucks free a loose tooth as a souvenir. Eventually, he amassed enough teeth for his signature shark-tooth necklace, a reminder of long-fought battles and the satisfaction of the release.

"Talk about adrenaline," he said. "Sticking your hand into the jaws of an angry tiger shark can really get your blood pumping."

What gets his blood pumping today is conservation. Sandifer is president and founder of Friends of Padre, a nonprofit group dedicated to cleaning up South Padre Island's Big Shell Beach. Sandifer, who was honored in 2009 as one of the country's conservation heroes, has won numerous recognitions for his work with injured wildlife, turtle restoration, and better beach access for those confined to wheelchairs.

But it was back in 1976 when Sandifer caught the first of his two biggest sharks from the beach.

"I was fishing alone on that trip. November seventh. I'd caught a lot of bait a few days earlier, too much to bring home, and so I decided to bury one of the thirty-pound jack crevalles in the sand. When I returned, I dug it up and used it as shark bait."

After rigging the rotting carcass with the huge hooks, Sandifer set the surf rod in its holder, set the free spool on clicker to avoid a backlash, and headed off in his dime-store inflatable dinghy with its plastic paddle and his shark bait, to spend the rest of the day fighting a stiff offshore breeze. It took him hours to reach his destination: one of the deep channels hundreds of yards from shore.

"I remember that long paddle out to the shark grounds, and the stink of the bait. There were maggots crawling all over it, and all over me. It was all I could do to get the bait out there without getting eaten alive by those things."

Sandifer returned to shore and waited, knowing it would take only a few hours for a big tiger to pick up the scent of the bait. When the shark struck, the rod tip heaved forward and the big reel roared its resistance with the familiar clack of the drag. Sandifer yanked

the rod from its holder and set the hook, and for an hour and a half, he battled the big fish. Eventually, Sandifer hauled the shark into shallow water, waded fearlessly to its side, and tail-roped it before towing it up the sand with his Suburban. The official weight back at the pier was 740 pounds. An impressive catch, but the monster shark was yet to come.

Fourteen years later, on November 10, 1990, Sandifer was fishing with friend and neighbor Charlie Krause.

"I remember it like it was yesterday," Krause told me. "It was not the kind of experience you ever forget."

They headed to Sandifer's favorite spot, where he'd caught his personal best 14 years earlier. Krause soon had a sack of 30-pound jacks, and by late afternoon, they were ready to fish.

"I cut the head off the big jack and rigged the body with two sixteen-ought hooks," Krause says. "I was using one-hundred-thirty-pound line on a twelve-inch Penn Senator reel. The leader was twenty feet of stainless steel aircraft cable, and I had six pounds of lead for weight. I used a one-man life raft to paddle out to the shark grounds. There wasn't any wind that day, so it didn't take long."

After setting the bait, Krause returned to shore and set the drag on the heavy-duty fishing rod set into a metal pipe welded to the back of Sandifer's Suburban.

"We rigged the rod holders so that the tips of the rods stuck up eighteen to twenty feet into the air. That way the line stayed above the surf and clear of the weeds and trash that washes up."

As the sun dropped low on the horizon, Krause's reel zippered loudly with the release of line. Krause freed the rod from its holder and leaned against the weight.

"At first it felt like the line had hung up on something, because it was so sluggish. The line went into the current and then back out. It took a while for me to realize how big a fish it was. The shark was so big it went anywhere it wanted at whatever pace it wanted."

Krause worked up and down the beach, at times entering the water up to his chest before working his way back to dry sand. As dusk settled over the beach, Krause hauled his catch into the shallows. Sandifer waded into the darkening water and gaffed his friend's record catch.

"When Billy tail-roped the shark, it looked like we'd captured a dinosaur," Krause said. "I'd never seen a fish so big up close like that. I sat with that shark all night in awe, waiting for the sun to rise before heading to the bait shop for an official weight. I spent the night just staring at its jaws and teeth. It was twelve feet long, and when I dug a trench around its body to get under its belly for a girth measurement, it came to seventy-eight and a half inches."

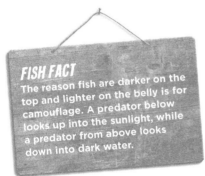

FISH FACT
The reason fish are darker on the top and lighter on the belly is for camouflage. A predator below looks up into the sunlight, while a predator from above looks down into dark water.

As the sun rose the next morning, the pair tried to load the shark into the back of the Suburban.

"We weren't prepared for such a big fish. We hunted the beach and found some rope and a six-by-six that we used to make a pulley. We found more wood to make a ramp up to the tailgate. We used PVC piping as rollers under the shark, then ran the six-by-six through the open windows of the front doors of the truck. It took longer to load it than it did to catch it."

Using a come-along, they slowly hitched the tiger shark up the ramp one inch at a time, and 4 hours later headed back to Corpus Christi. Word spread quickly as the Suburban drove through town with an enormous shark tail hanging from the back. By the time they reached Roy's Bait and Tackle, a large crowd had gathered. The shark was hoisted to the certified scale, where it weighed an astonishing 820 pounds. It was the largest fish ever caught from the surf.

"After the photos were taken, we took it back to the beach and cut out the jaws. Then we cleaned and gutted it and gave the meat to the local crab fishermen so that nothing got wasted."

Today the set of jaws hangs in Krause's living room as a reminder of a day unlike any other.

TRIPLE-DIGIT MARLIN FOR SINGLE-DIGIT KID

When Jonathan Curin was 4 years old, he practiced fishing for lunkers by reeling in his Labrador retriever. Close family friend and respected New Zealand boat captain Bill Hall would tie Jonathan's fishing line to the dog's collar and then set the drag on the reel loosely. Captain Hall would tell Jonathan to hang on just before he threw a bone across the yard. Three years later, at age 7, Jonathan said he was ready to go marlin fishing.

"I always wanted to catch a marlin," Curin said, "so my mum and I planned a trip to the Bay of Islands. Captain Hall was our captain, and for two days before we went fishing, he took me out to the bay to practice with a bucket. He would hook the bucket to the fishing line and drop it over the side of the boat and let it sink. The deeper it went, the heavier it got and the harder it was to reel up. It was good practice."

Early the next morning, Jonathan and crew left for Three Kings Islands, located 34 miles from the tip of northern New Zealand. The three small islands are home to some of the world's largest striped marlin. Fierce winds can often make the seas dangerous, but on this day, sky and sea were calm.

"It still took fourteen hours to get there," Curin said. "We saw lots of porpoises and feeding birds, and the whole time we talked about marlin."

The first day, Curin hooked a big marlin and fought it for an hour and a half before losing it at the boat. Disappointed, Curin went to bed early. He woke to another beautifully calm day, ready for action.

"The second day, I hooked another marlin, but after another hour or so, it spit the hook. I was mad, but I wanted to try again."

The fishing lines were reset when a dark spike broke the calm surface. Captain Hall raced to the cockpit and handed one of the two fishing rods to Curin, who settled into the fighting chair and attached the shoulder harness to the reel. Suddenly, two marlin appeared in the boat's wake. One attacked Curin's bait while the other hit the second trolled bait, which was fished by Captain Hall's wife, Robyn. Within seconds, both reels spun loudly as the marlin took line into the depths.

"Robyn fought her fish standing up," Curin said. "It was a big striped marlin, and when she got it to the boat, she tagged and released it. My stripy was still on, and it had jumped a few times. I was amazed at how big it was so I never stopped pulling."

The adult-size shoulder harness, however,

was too large for Curin's small shoulders and began to slip. A pillow was stuffed behind his back to keep it tight, but still it had to be adjusted throughout the fight.

"My mum and Robyn kept giving me drinks and food, and after an hour I had the marlin close to the boat. Captain Hall saw it coming and yelled to me to get ready. Then I saw them pulling it through the transom door. It was huge!"

The exhausted angler was congratulated, and Captain Hall turned for home. They drove through the night and arrived the next day at their homeport in the Bay of Islands. Curin's first marlin was hoisted to the scale, where it weighed an impressive 292 pounds.

"I was so tired the next day, I could barely lift my arms. But I was also excited. I got interviewed by local radio, and I was on the front page of the newspaper. I was even on the local television news."

The accomplishment was spectacular, but it paled in comparison to the marlin Curin caught the next year. At age 8, Curin was again fishing with Captain Hall when he landed a 450-pound blue marlin on 33-pound fishing line. That catch set a New Zealand line class record.

FISH FACT
Garfish have some of the toughest scales in the world. Native Americans used them as arrowheads.

"Captain Hall told me I was a good student," Curin said. "But I know I had the best teacher."

TWELVE HOURS, FOUR FISHING RODS, ONE EPIC MARLIN

Monday, September 8, the first day of fishing in the 26th Annual Marlin Fishing Tournament at Montego Bay, Jamaica, was destined to be a time that angler Headley Weir and the crew of the *Spritzer* would never forget.

Shortly after 9:00 a.m., Weir was in the fighting chair, solidly hooked to a big blue marlin on 50-pound-test fishing line packed onto a Penn 80 International reel holding 900 yards of monofilament. When the fish was near the boat, Captain Victor Murdock, a seasoned big game angler with more than 30 years of experience on the bridge, realized the size of their catch. The marlin appeared to be as long as the width of the 16-foot transom. A 1,062-pound marlin landed in Kona, Hawaii, had measured just over 14 feet.

Before the deckhand could reach out and wire it with the leader, the fish made a blistering run and stripped off most of the 900 yards of fishing line even with the boat backing down hard. The battle seesawed back and forth for the next 6 hours. Each time the anglers pulled him in, the fish raced away, nearly spooling the reel each time. By mid-afternoon, the seas had built

FISH FACT
Baby salmon, called smolts or alevins, swim downstream tail-first.

to 8 feet, and on one of the long runs, with Captain Murdock backing down fast, the swimming platform was ripped loose.

On the next run, the big blue made it obvious that 900 yards of line was insufficient. As Weir watched the last few yards melt from the spool, the crew snapped the swivel of a 10/0 reel with 80-pound-test fishing line to Weir's reel and dropped the original rod and reel overboard.

Weir continued to fight the fish on the 10/0 rig, knowing that the second set of gear would disqualify the fish from the tournament. Nevertheless, all on board wanted to land the fish to confirm its massive size. Using a second rod clipped to the reel of the first rod had worked for Captain Murdock before, so expectations were high.

As the fight entered the seventh and then the eighth hour, Weir was able to regain his first fishing rod and reel and most of the 900 yards of line. But the marlin soon took the upper hand and the second rod was once again attached. The big marlin continued to run, and soon a third rod and reel was snapped to the second reel, which was summarily tossed overboard. The fight continued, with two sets of gear in the water trailing behind the fish.

The tournament had by now ended for the day, and the cocktail party was in full force back at the Montego Bay Yacht Club. But many crew members from the other boats stayed close to their marine radios to monitor the epic battle taking place a few miles away.

As Weir, an experienced angler, watched the sun set, he was determined to keep fighting. But as darkness fell, the fish seemed to gain strength. It ran harder and harder, and soon a fourth rod and reel was attached and the third set of gear was dumped overboard. With three expensive and heavy rods and reels in the water, and a combined total of approximately 2,500 yards of line trailing behind the fish, the fish sounded. Backing down on the fish became impossible. The location of the marlin was indeterminable.

Weir continued to fight gallantly, but he was unable to stop the loss of fishing line. The marlin kept swimming, and at the 12-hour mark, a fifth rod and reel was snapped into place, secured to a double 50-pound line. The effort was futile, however, as the fish never stopped.

Finally, the great marlin, pulling four rods and reels and finishing off 4,000 yards of fishing line, succeeded in forcing Weir to tighten the drag. The line snapped and the fight was over. Gone was the fish, 2 miles of line, and four sets of fishing gear.

We can only hope that somewhere in the darkness of night, the mighty marlin was able to break loose from her burden and swim free.

VORACIOUS MARLIN

It was Friday the 13th when Michael Nebsbit and Bryan Toney hooked a fat billfish from the deck of the 17-foot *Felicidad* off the coast of Kona, Hawaii. The big fish fought for 2 hours, then it spit out the 40-pound aku bait. The aku floated to the surface, but the marlin was unfazed by the previous battle. It turned and charged the bait, re-hooking itself for a second time. Unfortunately, the reel froze. The anglers, who were both experienced charter boat mates, cut the line and spliced it to a second reel. Within minutes the second reel broke, forcing the men to hand-line the estimated 500-pound blue marlin. One man pulled on the monofilament, while the other used his finger to crank the broken reel. Somehow, they were able to land the fish. Not only was landing such a large marlin by hand improbable, but it was the first time either man had heard of a marlin returning to attack a bait rigged with a sharp hook after such a long fight. Then again, it was Friday the 13th.

FISH FACT
The age of a fish is calculated by growth rings on its scales. Each ring equals one year.

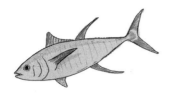

NOT-SO-MELLOW YELLOWFIN

Eleven-year-old Clayton Ludington joined his dad aboard the 115-foot *Royal Polaris* in San Diego, California, for a 17-day fishing trip. They were headed to Clarion Island, a fish-rich oasis 500 miles south of Cabo San Lucas, Mexico. It was an epic trip from the start, and by the time Clayton had reached Clarion, he'd bagged countless tuna, a large wahoo, and a sailfish.

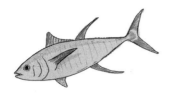

FISH FACT
The longest jellyfish to ever wash ashore landed at Cape Ann, Massachusetts. It measured 245 feet from head to tail.

"When we got to the island," Clayton said, "I pinned a big *caballito* baitfish on my hook and cast it out. The tuna were biting, and after about fifteen minutes, the *caballito* really started swimming. I knew something was chasing it. I had about a hundred yards of line out when the big fish hit."

The hooked tuna surged for the ocean floor, burning Clayton's fingers on the free-spooling reel. Clayton locked the drag and set the hook. The fish swam deep, taking line effortlessly. For ten minutes, Clayton struggled to hang on. He kept the rod tight in the gimbal of the waist belt, and leaned against the weight of the fish. As his arms tired, he handed the rod to the deckhand and grabbed a harness. The deckhand clipped the rod into the harness and handed it to Clayton, who could now lean back without using his arms. It was a powerful fish, and more than once it slammed Clayton to the railing, where he rested the rod and waited for the fish to tire.

An hour and 10 minutes later, the fish began to rise. The deckhands called out for extra gaffs. It was the largest yellowfin tuna Clayton had ever seen.

"It took five gaffs to land the tuna," he said, "and a bunch of the deckhands to lift it over the railing. I couldn't believe how big it was."

Days later, back at the dock in San Diego, the fish was officially weighed. It registered 315 pounds and was the largest tuna of the trip. It was also the largest tuna ever caught by such a young angler in the San Diego fleet. In fact, it was one of the largest tuna ever caught by any angler in the fleet.

"Three-hundred-pound tuna are why anglers book our trips," Captain Frank LoPreste, owner of the *Royal Polaris*, said. "Clayton is an exceptionally tough eleven-year-old fisherman. He hung in there and landed what will probably turn out to be the greatest fish of his life."

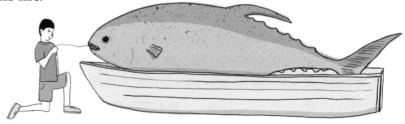

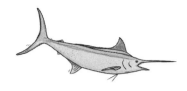

THE FOX AND THE MARLIN

Captain George "The Fox" Bransford had retired from big game fishing by the time I drove down his driveway in central Queensland, Australia. Originally from Florida, Bransford had spent a lifetime as a professional skipper, fishing much of the world. "The Fox" was a legend. He had been for a long time.

The successful capture of Australia's first 1,000-pound fish—a "grander"—began by chance during World War II, when Bransford was an American paratrooper stationed in the small town of Gordonvale on the northeast coast of Australia. On training missions high above the sea, he began to study the Great Barrier Reef. A fisherman by trade, Bransford was intrigued by the stark blue line that marked the edge of the great reef. It was there, he believed, that the warm currents of the ocean would mix with the rich waters of the reef, creating ideal conditions for game fish—lots of them.

At every opportunity, he went to the seaside town of Cairns, where the reef was nearest to shore. He watched the local mackerel boats return from fishing, and he talked with their captains. They all complained about the same thing: big menacing fish that

Captain George Bransford (left) and Richie Obach with the first Australian grander caught with a rod and reel

attacked their mackerel. It was just what Bransford had guessed. He vowed to return one day to pursue a dream.

Twenty years later, in 1964, Bransford returned. He had sold his home in the States, moved his family, and staked it all on finding these fish. He needed results. He began searching the inner reefs for billfish. He started up a small charter business, but times were tough and the fishing was slow.

Late that year, on November 25, he caught a 35-pound black marlin. Then in early 1965, his wife, Joyce, caught the largest marlin ever landed in Australia, a 252-pound black marlin. The catch was enough to stir a local interest in their budding charter business, the first of its kind along the coast.

On September 28, 1965, almost a year after landing his first black marlin, Bransford and his deckhand, Richie Obach, navigated their way toward the outer waters far beyond the reef. It was a day free of charters, a day for exploring new ground. Their destination was the edge of the reef, the Continental Shelf, more than 30 miles from the coast. Fresh baits were rigged and skipped along the water's surface, but by early afternoon, the only fish in the box were mackerel, trevally, and barracuda.

Then from beneath the water came a huge black bill. "Marlin! Port 'rigger," hollered Bransford. His heart raced as the fish slapped the bait with terrific force. The 80-pound line snapped from the outrigger clip and spun from the reel. The marlin's body shuddered, then disappeared beneath the water.

Immediately the sea erupted. The marlin rocketed from the surface, thrusting its head from side to side to escape the jab of the hook. Repeatedly it charged the surface, and repeatedly the reel shrieked. Obach held the rod and followed Bransford's commands. He was young and strong, and eager to catch the monster fish.

"Don't let him rest!" Branford yelled. "Give it all you've got. More pressure, Richie—now's when you need to give him hell. Don't give him an inch!"

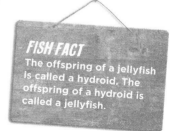

FISH FACT

The offspring of a jellyfish is called a hydroid. The offspring of a hydroid is called a jellyfish.

Together they worked, constantly talking, always alert. It was 2 hours before the fish tired. Obach pulled one last time and the leader hit the rod tip. He slid the rod into its holder and dug a gaff deep into the fish.

It was big, at least 700 or 800 pounds. They tried to pull it into the cockpit, but its size was too great. Their only choice was to tie it off the stern and tow it to shore.

Night had fallen, so the treacherous trip home had to be navigated by moonlight. Slowly, weaving through the lattice of shallow reefs, they made their way to the dock. It had been 2 hours since they reported their catch, and a large crowd was waiting. But it was late and the scales were closed. They put the fish in a makeshift freezer. The final weight would be delayed until morning.

At daybreak, the marlin was trucked across town to the certified scales located at the railroad station. The crowd had returned and whooped happily as the scales reached 1,064 pounds. It was the first grander ever caught in Australia and a new world record. The black marlin measured nearly 14 feet from bill to tail and had a girth of 81 inches.

The gamble had paid off. Bransford's dream had come true.

BETTER LIVING THROUGH BASS FISHING

"One more for good luck!" Dave Romeo shouted to the crowd lining the shores of Kahler's Pond, Long Island, New York. It was the afternoon of October 28, 1984, the last day of fishing season. Romeo, who had already caught 3,000 largemouth bass that season, flipped up the tip of his fishing rod and set the hook on his 3,001st. He played it for a few extra minutes, enjoying his moment of glory.

Mobs of media had joined the lakeside crowd to witness and record Romeo's final bass of the year. A smile stretched across Romeo's face as he bent down to release the fish. He had shattered all previous estimates of a single-season catch. Names like "Bass Master" and "the Babe Ruth of Bass Fishing" would become common sobriquets for this 25-year-old tax consultant.

But Romeo was not your average fisherman. He was devoted to, almost obsessed with, better fishing. He had devoted 3 years to studying the art of bass fishing, keeping a detailed record of every bass he caught, including dates, times, locations, weather patterns, baits, and lures.

"There had to be reasons for fish to bite," Romeo explained.

"Certain days were better than others. My goal was to figure out why."

He read every bass fishing book available, searching for new strategies and new techniques. The best advice came from Robert Deindorfer's *Positive Fishing: The Art of Angling to Your Outer Limit*, whose central theme was concentration—the more concentration you had, the more fish you would catch.

"I broke the thousand mark by June," Romeo said, "and knew I could double it by the end of the season. I wanted the people at Guinness to recognize the record, but they were hesitant. So I got on the phone and contacted everyone with a vested interest in the record. Every fishing company whose tackle I was using sent letters on my behalf. I also sent in all the

Guinness record holder Dave Romeo and a few of his 3,001 bass

media coverage I'd received to verify my claim to the record."

Fourteen hours every weekend day, every vacation day, and every day off, Romeo searched for bass. He weathered the cold, the rain, and the wind. He ate little, resting only to switch lures or change locations. Though a dedicated angler, he missed only one day of work the entire 3-month season. Fishing from inflatable rafts, small boats, and shorelines, Romeo averaged 38 to 40 bass a day for 77 days. All but 28 of the 3,001 fish were released; some were caught more than once, while one was caught more than six times.

Romeo became a hometown hero. He even wrote a book, *Better Bass Fishing, the Dave Romeo Way*, and founded a family-style catch-and-release bass tournament that bears his name.

One more thing. During his quest for the record, he met his future wife. Her name? Kim Trout.

FISH FACT

Anemone fish, as well as the popular clown fish, are sequential hermaphrodites, which means when the dominant female is gone from the school, the largest male will take her place—and undergo a sex change to become female. Other fish, like wrasses and groupers, begin life as males but may change to females later in life.

WHEN IN DOUBT, PADDLE OUT

When Dr. Hal Neibling and Curt Herberts left the harbor at Mexico's famed Cabo San Lucas, little did they know they were about to make billfishing history—of a sort.

They were aboard Lee Stockland's sleek sportfisher *Tio Lee*, skippered by Randy Wood. It was 10:00 in the morning, and they were drift fishing for marlin 2 miles from shore. Neibling was fishing from the bow, Herberts from the stern.

Suddenly, both anglers hooked up. Herberts's fish crashed through the surface, leaping and splashing its way due south. Niebling's fish did the same, except it headed due north.

Wood didn't move the boat. Instead, he hurried down from the bridge and raced inside the cabin. He found the board portion of a Windsurfer he carried for windy days, rushed out to the deck, and dropped it into the water. Seconds later, Neibling scrambled over the transom, straddled the board, and sailed across the water after his marlin. Wood hurried back to the bridge and reversed the engines, leaving Neibling alone on a narrow board being pulled by an angry marlin.

Meanwhile, Herberts's fish was more than 300 yards away and still taking line. "I couldn't put much pressure on the twenty-pound line," he said afterward. "But once we started to follow the fish, it turned and headed back at us. I quickly regained a hundred yards of line and things were looking up. Except when we turned to find Hal, and he was gone."

The marlin had pulled Neibling away from the *Tio Lee* and was towing him out to sea. A breeze had begun to blow, creating an afternoon chop, but Neibling, who was wearing a life jacket, calmly fought his fish. Several small *pangas* and Mexican sportfishers circled in the distance, keeping him within sight.

"Those people must have thought I was crazy," Neibling said, "but it was all pretty easy. I kept my feet in the water for balance and the drag on the reel set loose. The marlin did most of the work, pulling me along, tiring himself out. The only frightening moment was when I thought about sharks. I decided to put my feet on top of the board, and I nearly capsized. Needless to say, it was the last time I thought about sharks."

As Herberts's fish neared the boat, Stan Grier, another angler on board, scanned the horizon with binoculars and eventually spotted Neibling more than a mile away. Herberts tagged his fish and then went after Neibling. They were reunited 45 minutes after Neibling first took off after the marlin.

FISH FACT
The freshwater priapus fish has its urinary, anal, and reproductive organs at the front of its body near its head and gill plates.

Neiblung's marlin, now exhausted, hovered 30 feet below the water. Neibling was elated. Everyone on the *Tio Lee* offered encouragement as he asked for the tagging stick. He pulled the marlin close to the board, seized the leader in one hand, tied the rod to a trailing rope, and tagged the fish 1 inch ahead and 2 inches to the right of the dorsal fin. Herberts tossed him a pocketknife, and Neibling cut the leader. He paddled to the boat, climbed onto the deck, and asked for the coldest beer in the cooler.

Dr. Hal Neibling fighting an estimated 150-pound striped marlin from a Windsurfer miles from the coast of Cabo San Lucas, Mexico

BLUEFIN TUNA WRESTLING

John Malandra was surf fishing the shores of Brant Beach, New Jersey, not far from Atlantic City, when he hooked a 179-pound bluefin tuna. Malandra had fought the huge tuna all the way to shore, when his line snapped. Onlookers watched in disbelief as Malandra dropped his gear and charged into the surf. For 15 minutes, he wrestled with the slippery brute, refusing to lose his once-in-a-lifetime catch.

Eventually, someone in the crowd tossed him a beach towel, which Malandra used to wrap the fish's tail and tow it onto dry sand. It was the largest tuna ever caught from the New Jersey surf, where on average, surf fishermen catch tuna in the 20- to 30-pound range.

FISH FACT
Juvenile batfish, tripletails, and filefishes evade predators by mimicking dead leaves as they float about in sargassum weed.

CAPSIZED CAPTURE

"**M**ayday! Mayday! We're sinking!" Mele Akaka cried into the radio, straining her eyes toward shore. Volcanic ash from Mauna Loa choked the air, obscuring the rocky coastline. "We're five miles from the airport, five miles from the trees on the hill, five miles from . . ."

A large wave smashed the side of the 17-foot skiff, shifting Akaka's catch—a 391-pound blue marlin and 100 pounds of aku—to one side and flinging Akaka to the deck. The two fish were tied to the boat, but the waves were so strong they were shifting them from side to side and tilting the boat dangerously. Five-foot seas slammed into the stern, sloshing water over the transom. The captain, who had been switching fuel tanks, struggled desperately to connect the fuel hose.

"We were dead in the water," Akaka said afterward, "and the fish in the boat were tilting us to one side. I felt us move backward, and looked up to see a huge blue marlin lying on the water. He had one of our lures in his mouth and was just playing with it. The reel never made a sound. We just started moving backward. The marlin was pulling us, unconcerned about the waves or the two huge fish on board."

Moving uncontrollably in large waves proved to be a dangerous combination. Before Akaka or the captain could cut the fishing line, the playful marlin changed course, turning the boat sideways into the swells. Seconds later, the skiff capsized.

Captain Chuck Harlin and his son, Captain Mike Harlin, were miles away, fishing with clients aboard their 36-foot charter boat *Kealia*. The guests that day were Congressman Joseph Kennedy III of Massachusetts, Congressman Bart Gordon of Tennessee, and two retired football players, John Wilber of the Washington Redskins and Houston Oiler Scott Collins. Also aboard were Kennedy's twin sons, Little Joe and Matthew. The fishing on the *Kealia* had been slow all morning, when Akaka's distress call came over the radio.

"She was understandably frantic," Chuck Harlin said, "and her locations were confusing. She gave three or four different headings. The chances of finding her were pretty remote. I turned and headed toward the closest location she gave."

Eventually, the elder Harlin glimpsed a small white dot on the horizon and veered toward it. Along the way, a fish breached near the dot and crashed back into the sea. As they approached, they could see the rounded frame of the boat bobbing on the surface.

It had been 45 minutes since Akaka's plea for help, and now two bodies clung desperately to the vertical shaft of the outboard motor.

Harlin, Kennedy, and Collins dove into the water and swam to the rescue. They helped Akaka to the *Kealia*, then returned to the

FISH FACT
Frogfish are strange-looking creatures that resemble a sea sponge, and instead of a dorsal fin, they come equipped with a natural fishing lure that dangles from their foreheads to attract prey into their bucket mouths.

overturned boat. Kennedy donned a scuba mask and dove below the surface to try and salvage some gear. Five hundred pounds of dead fish awaited him.

Kennedy's alarm on seeing the marlin was understandable. "It was the biggest fish he had ever seen, and he was worried about sharks," said Akaka.

Kennedy dove back beneath the boat. A lone rod dangled upside down from the stern, secured to the railing by a safety cord. The limp fishing line trailed out into the blueness, its hook out of sight. Kennedy unhooked the safety cord and swam the rod and reel to the *Kealia*, where Wilber was waiting.

Wilber began to reel the slack line, when suddenly it tightened and angled toward the surface. Moments later, a blue marlin surged from below, thrashing its head in defiance. The fish that had capsized the boat an hour earlier was still hooked!

Akaka tried to land the fish, but the marlin dove deep, became tail-wrapped, and died. Mike Harlin, who had returned from the capsized boat, hand-lined the dead fish to the boat.

Meanwhile, a local boat, *Notorious*, had arrived and its crew helped right the capsized boat. They tied a rope to the skiff's bow and towed her to harbor. Akaka remained aboard the *Kealia* and returned with her fish and the crew that had saved her life.

SHOCKING ACTS OF FISH AGGRESSION

HOOK IN MOUTH DISEASE

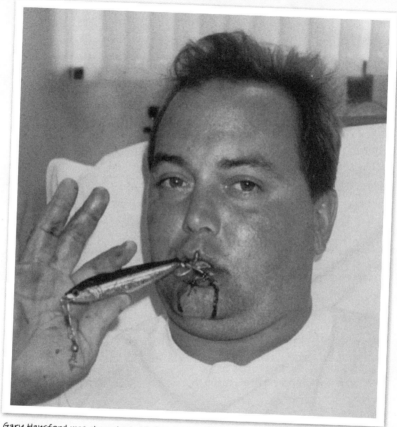

Gary Hansford was aboard a half-day fishing boat out of southern California when he was hooked by a fellow angler who was overhand-casting from the stern of the boat.

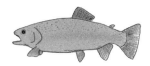

FLESH-EATING TROUT

Mark Blackstone had fished Priest Lake, Idaho, for decades. The fish grow big in that part of northern Idaho, and the deepwater lake remains cold most of the year—cold enough to preserve logs and dead animals, and even the occasional body lurking beneath the lake's surface.

"One time while fishing a steep drop-off, I snagged something heavy," he said, "but it fell off, and when I brought up the lure, one of the hooks had a piece of skin with eyelashes on it. My buddies and I thought it was from a deer and so we threw it back. Later we heard that a man had drowned near where we were fishing, but they never recovered the body."

Blackstone, who lives in Idaho, continued to fish Priest Lake, returning every year to his favorite fishing holes, often limiting on fat mackinaw trout. Then on September 11, 2012, Blackstone and his brother, Mike, and good friend Calvin Nolan caught a trout with a strange roll to its belly.

"It was an eight-pound mackinaw," Blackstone said. "Since we had a six-fish limit, we kept it. Later when we were filleting our catch for the day, we noticed that this one's belly was puffed out. Calvin cut it open and saw what he thought looked like a crawfish in there. But Mike said, 'It looks like a . . . finger!' "

It wasn't a crawfish. As the anglers looked closer, they noticed the object had joints and a fingernail. "It was perfectly preserved," Blackstone said. "Someone had lost his pinkie just below the second joint. We weren't sure what to do, or if there was a body down there or maybe more parts. We thought about going back to the spot, which we had marked on our GPS, but it was late and the sun was going down. Plus, it was a spot that dropped down to a hundred and thirty feet, so there wasn't much we could do."

Instead, they checked the bellies of their other fish, and then called the local sheriff's department. The deputy filed the report, but because of the late hour and the remote location of the anglers on the lake, the deputy told them to keep the finger on ice until morning.

"We placed the pinkie in a baggie and put it in our cooler overnight along with all the fish fillets. We talked about what we thought might have happened, whether someone had been killed and dumped in the lake, or if it was a drowning victim. I know none of us slept very well that night."

The next morning, the sheriff's deputy arrived, and the finger was catalogued and printed. It was also quickly identified. Two months earlier, a tourist named Haans Galassi had been wakeboarding on Priest Lake when an accident had occurred. Haans was in the water, positioned on the board, ready for the heavy tug of the boat, when the towrope wrapped around his hand and cinched tight, cutting off the end two joints of all four fingers of his left hand. The lost digits sank to the bottom of the cold lake, where they remained until Blackstone's mackinaw trout swam by.

"The spot where we caught the trout," Blackstone said, "was about eight miles from where the man had lost his fingers. That's a long way for a trout to swim, and the finger was so well pre-served that it couldn't have been in the fish's belly very long. So either the fish ate it and swam the eight miles or deepwater currents car-ried it down the lake. When I talked with the local Fish and Game official, he thought it was incredible that a trout could swim that far that fast."

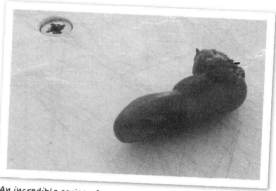

An incredible series of events led to finding this finger in the belly of a trout.

"I heard that the guy told the sheriff to keep the finger. He didn't want it back. I guess I wouldn't want it back either, but I was glad to hear he was alive."

As difficult as this fishing story is to believe, finding a human body part in a lake fish has happened before. You'll find it in the story titled "Thumbing for Trout."

WHAT GOES UP MUST COME DOWN

George Williams and Tommy Thompson, both members of the Southern California Tuna Club, were fishing off Dana Point one summer, when a marlin they had hooked provided some unexpected "entertainment."

"Tommy hooked the marlin the minute his bait hit the water," Williams said. "But the fish only jumped once, refused to fight, and then came straight to the boat. I wanted no part of a green billfish, so I drove forward and had Tommy work on him some more."

Williams, still wary of the fish, put the boat in gear and spun out another few hundred yards of line. "The marlin must have liked us," Williams continued, "because he turned right around and swam back. Tommy had been complaining about my moving the boat and threatened to throw the gear overboard if I didn't gaff the marlin. I was feeling bad about it myself, so I jumped into the cockpit and readied the gaff.

"As soon as I grabbed the leader, the marlin came to life and jumped

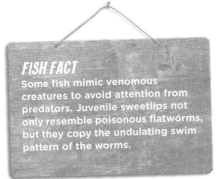

FISH FACT
Some fish mimic venomous creatures to avoid attention from predators. Juvenile sweetlips not only resemble poisonous flatworms, but they copy the undulating swim pattern of the worms.

straight up out of the water, brushing the side of the boat. He looked like a missile coming out of the ocean. I yelled to Tommy and ducked."

But Thompson didn't duck. Instead, as the marlin went up, he reached out and snatched it by the bill. The momentum and speed of the fish carried him up off the deck and into the air.

"I've seen a marlin jump pretty high," Williams said, "but not with a two-hundred-pound man hanging on. They went at least another six feet off the deck before they crashed down inside the cockpit."

Thompson's shoulder was dislocated and he couldn't move. The marlin, now corralled in the boat, flopped and thrashed across the deck. Williams ran to Thompson, lifted him by the shirt, and dragged him up to the bridge.

"We waited for the fish to calm down," Williams said, "and then headed in. It wasn't the easiest way to catch a marlin, but it was certainly one of the most memorable."

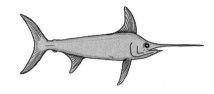

PINNED BY A SWORDFISH

Mexican *pangero* Jose Rojas Mayarita was fishing along from his canoelike craft miles off the Pacific Coast of Mexico, when the swordfish he was hand-lining rocketed from the water. The 10-foot-long billfish soared overhead, before diving directly into Rojas Mayarita's midsection. The tip of the serrated sword traveled through the man's stomach and continued through the wooden hull, pinning both man and fish to the boat. The swordfish soon died, but the badly wounded Rojas Mayarita was unable to free himself from the fish or the boat. For two days he floated at sea, sure to die, when he was discovered by another *pangero*. The shocked *pangero* towed the wounded man and his *panga* to Acapulco, where he was cut free and rushed to one of the local hospitals. Staff physician Dr. David Mendoza Millan reported that Rojas Mayarita miraculously survived.

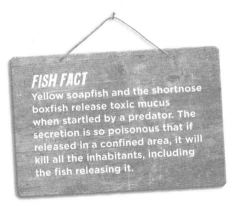

FISH FACT
Yellow soapfish and the shortnose boxfish release toxic mucus when startled by a predator. The secretion is so poisonous that if released in a confined area, it will kill all the inhabitants, including the fish releasing it.

BUSHWHACKED BY WHALES

Imagine it's your first big game fishing trip. You've just hooked your first marlin, a whopper. Your adrenaline is flowing, your heart is racing, and everyone on board is whooping and hollering in celebration.

You settle in for the fight. You hope nothing goes wrong. The hook, the line, the reel . . . the whales?

It was a warm January day, and Joe Nangle and his father, Paul, had chartered a local fishing boat, *E-Ka-Mo-Na*, at Hawaii's Honokohau Harbor just outside Kona. The skipper, John Llanes, welcomed the two anglers aboard, and within the hour was working the usual fishing grounds. The surface was calm, when suddenly, 60 yards away, a pod of pilot whales surfaced. The whales were feeding, and Llanes veered to head them off.

"Marlin!" he shouted from the bridge.

The rod dipped and the engines roared. Joe Nangle leaped into the chair and set the hook on his first marlin—a big one. Her enormous body broke through the surface and soared into the air. She twisted and shook and splashed heavily on the water. She hurled herself upward again and again, each time landing with great force. The captain and crew shouted their approval, estimating her weight at more than 700 pounds. The whales, meanwhile, lolled nearby.

The marlin sounded, and for the next hour Nangle steadily worked the rod, eager to land the trophy fish. The whales continued to linger, docile and seemingly uninterested in the battle. Then without warning, they charged.

The exhausted marlin made a desperate plunge for the ocean floor. Line spun from the reel at a blistering pace. The whirling spool became too hot to touch. Nangle watched helplessly as the fishing line he had worked so hard to retrieve faded into blue water. Then it was over. The reel quieted and the line stopped. They knew that the marlin had ruptured her air bladder and drowned in the depths.

Relieved to still have weight on his line, Nangle began retrieving his catch. Twenty minutes passed. Then, as the silhouette of the marlin began to emerge, so did the whales. Only this time they were closer.

Nangle reeled frantically with all his strength until the swivel cleared the water. The deckhand reached out, palmed the leader, and wrapped it around his hand. He had pulled the marlin within gaffing range, when suddenly a huge bull whale appeared beneath the boat. The whale charged the dead marlin, clamping it in its jaws, then turned and raced away from the boat.

The reel spun uncontrollably, and Nangle began to unsnap the harness. But the whale surfaced, stopped swimming, and shook the huge marlin in the air like a sardine. Other whales rushed in for the feast, and within seconds, Nangle's catch was reduced to blood and foam.

FISH FACT

Porcupine fish are covered in spiny body armor and puff up like a spiked ball when confronted. This doesn't faze the mahi mahi. Several have been caught by anglers with bellies full of porcupine fish.

The sound of gunshots filled the air. Fearing for their safety, the captain had fired warning shots to frighten the whales away. Though illegal, the tactic worked and the whales sank below the surface. Quickly, Nangle hauled in all that remained of his marlin—180 pounds of head and trailing stomach. The scraps were brought aboard, and Llanes drove ahead at medium speed.

But like a pack of angry wolves, the whales resurfaced and rushed toward the boat. Unwilling to shoot directly at them, Llanes ordered the marlin head and remains thrown overboard and slammed down the throttles. The boat lurched forward, and as the remnants of Nangle's first marlin faded into the sea, the whales disappeared.

Llanes never slowed his course. The fishing was done for the day, but the story is one for the ages.

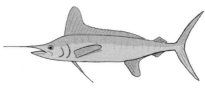

EN GARDE!

When Bob Fitzgerald was speared in the leg by a white marlin, he wasn't thinking about being lucky—but that's just what he was.

"My wife, Jane, and I were fishing off Andros Island in the Bahamas," Fitzgerald explained, "with Mike and Sunny Wirtz, owners of the ninety-one-foot yacht *Blackhawk*, and our friends Bob and Barbara Carlson. It was eleven in the morning, and I had just caught our first marlin of the trip. I stayed in the fighting chair and waited for one of the crew members to gaff the fish and bring him aboard."

It was a small white marlin, exhausted by the fight. But as it cleared the stern, the weary fish unexpectedly came to life. "I remember seeing the fish come over the transom and flip into the air. One minute he was calm, and the next minute he was a wild animal heading straight for me. It happened so fast, I couldn't get out of the chair. I just jerked to the side as far as I could and covered my face with my arms."

FISH FACT
Razorfish and seamoths resemble alien insects, but they are all fish—with fins and gills.

The marlin crashed into the boat, driving its bill through Fitzgerald's thigh. Everyone on board watched in horror as the fish ripped its bill from his leg and flopped wildly about the deck.

"As the bill came out," Fitzgerald said, "the barbs pulled muscle out through the hole. It was terrible to look at, but it plugged the wound and stopped the bleeding."

Everyone in the cockpit scrambled for cover while the captain radioed for help.

"There were some doctors around," Captain Hillard Hardy recalled, "but they were out fishing and wouldn't be back at the dock until late that afternoon. We cleaned the wound and turned toward shore, but Bob insisted we stay out so the rest of the gang could fish. I didn't like it, but he was adamant. The leg seemed okay, so we moved him to the upper deck and kept close watch over him in case the wound got any worse. Bob was a good patient. All he wanted was a fresh martini and some more fishing."

The decision turned out to be a good one. Sunny and Jane hooked into a double strike, and Mike landed a large blue marlin. Fitzgerald, his leg numb and swollen, watched from above, nursing martinis and cheering his friends' good fortune.

But by the time they arrived at the docks, Fitzgerald's leg was too stiff to move. Dr. Gordon Hill, an orthopedic surgeon from Miami, had been informed of the injury and was waiting at the dock.

"The leg was badly bruised and was bleeding internally," Hill said, "but the major arteries and the bone were not damaged. He was very fortunate."

Imagine having a fish like this on your line, and then having its bill spear into your leg!

Hill cleaned the wound, administered antibiotics and painkillers, and suggested that Fitzgerald get medical attention in the United States. After a day at sea and a long flight from the Bahamas to Illinois, Fitzgerald arrived in Chicago and went immediately to his own physician, Dr. Blazek. By then, the leg had turned dark purple.

"Had the marlin hit his femoral artery," Blazek said, "Bob could have lost his leg and possibly his life. There would have been no way to stop the massive bleeding that would have ensued. A tourniquet would have been his only chance."

After weeks of therapy, Fitzgerald's leg healed. Now, years later, all that remains is a small scar with a great story worthy of Hemingway himself.

SPEARED THROUGH THE CHEST

Captain Alan Card had been fishing the waters around Bermuda since the age of five, and by his early twenties, he had his own sportfishing boat and was soon booking charters and winning tournaments. On this day—standard by every measure—he expected to land the big marlin his client had hooked. He knew the marlin was big. Not grander big, but close.

"It was just like any other tournament," Captain Card said. "We were hooked up to a good fish and Ian was in the cockpit getting things ready."

Ian Card has worked with his father for more than 20 years as first mate and deckhand, landing seven granders over the years. He was there when they won the 1993 Blue Marlin World Cup Championship with a 1,195-pound blue that remains the record to this day. Ian has been there for the countless line-class world records landed aboard their 40-foot charter boat *Challenger*. Everything from yellowfin tuna to blackfin tuna and amberjack. But it was a day in July 2006 that stood apart from all others.

"I was at the controls," Captain Card said, "when without warning the marlin jumped. Most marlin jump away from the boat,

but this one came over the footrest of the fighting chair right where Ian was standing. It was fast and unexpected."

Ian never knew what hit him. The marlin punched a golf-ball-size hole through Ian's chest and continued over the opposite side of the boat and into the water, burying Ian beneath its 800-pound girth.

"The next thing I knew," Captain Card continued, "Ian was in the water upside down with this big marlin on top of him. Then he disappeared."

What happened next is nothing short of miraculous. Seconds later, Ian surfaced two boat lengths behind the *Challenger*, while the marlin, still hooked, sounded for the bottom of the Atlantic Ocean. Captain Card ordered the line cut and backed the boat down on his son.

FISH FACT
There are more than 25,000 species of fish.

"When we got him aboard, I could see the wound to his chest. It was just below his collarbone. I knew it was bad so I called for an ambulance and turned for home. Luckily one of our guests had some emergency medical training and he kept pressure on the wound."

Forty minutes later, the *Challenger* arrived

at the dock. Paramedics rushed Ian to the hospital, where doctors performed life-saving surgery.

"They told me later," Captain Card said, "that they could see the main artery coming from his heart. It was millimeters from getting punctured. If the marlin's bill had hit that artery, he would have bled out in minutes."

Ian spent 10 days in the hospital, and within months was back fishing with his dad.

The crew of the Challenger and their 1,195-pound marlin.

"We were lucky," Captain Card said. "It could have been an older person standing there or a kid, but it was Ian. He's a powerful guy and he survived. That day was unforgettable. I think about it all the time. Marlin fishing is exciting, but it's also unpredictable. I wouldn't want it any other way."

You can find Captain Card on Facebook at Challenger Charter Fishing, Bermuda.

SNAKE ON THE BOAT!

Kevin Jones and his fishing partner, Paul Shepherd, were anxious to catch their second bass of the day. It was early morning, and the two anglers were contestants in the American Bass Association's Team Tournament held at Castaic Lake in southern California. Shepherd had caught their first bass, a qualifying 3½-pound largemouth that was promptly placed in the boat's live well.

"We were feeling pretty good," Jones said. "It was still early in the morning, and we had a good fish in the live well. We needed five more to make the limit, so we headed into a nearby cove to see what we could find."

Shepherd stood at the bow, controlling the boat with the foot pedal and fishing a spinner bait. Jones was at the stern, working a crankbait deep. Slowly they fished the water and moved deeper and deeper into the cove.

"I caught a dink," Jones said, "probably no more than ten inches long, and as I released it I heard a splash near the shore. I thought maybe Paul had hooked a fish. When I looked up toward the bank, which was about fifty feet away, I saw something in the water. It was moving and coming our way."

Jones made another cast, and Shepherd hollered, "Snake!" Expecting Shepherd to move the boat elsewhere, Jones quickly reeled in his lure. Instead, Shepherd calmly resumed fishing.

FISH FACT
The largest freshwater fish is the Chinese paddlefish, which can grow to over 20 feet in length and weigh more than 1,600 pounds.

"Paul is from Oregon," Jones said, "and he had dealt with snakes before, so I figured he knew what he was doing. I decided not to worry about it. I needed another cast, and suddenly Paul said in a tense voice, 'Kevin, that's a rattlesnake!'"

Shepherd quickly reeled in his fishing line and changed the course of the boat away from the snake. Jones also retrieved his line and remained at the stern, nervously watching the rattlesnake.

"He was about twenty-five feet from us when we changed course," Jones said, "and he changed course right with us. Paul got a little nervous and hit the trolling motor to full speed. I thought that would do it, but within seconds the snake was right next to the boat."

Jones raised his expensive brass rod and thrashed at the water between the rattlesnake and the boat. But the snake was not deterred. "He wrapped himself around our big engine, and I was sure he wanted inside the boat. Paul was worried, too. He kept yelling, 'Don't let that snake on this boat!'"

Jones tossed his pole aside and grabbed the fishnet. He swung the net like a baseball bat but couldn't hit the snake.

"He was curled down in a little crevice," Jones said, "and I couldn't quite get at him. Finally I got brave and moved in close. I stood on the step near the back of the boat and poked the handle of the net into his body, and each time he would strike out and try to bite it."

Panicked and frustrated, Jones reared back and jabbed down hard at the snake. As the net came down, his foot slipped and he fell to the floor of the boat less than a foot from the snake's head. He was down for only a second, but he could see the snake looking right at him. "He struck out at my face, but he was coiled so tightly around the engine cables that he couldn't get any distance on his strikes."

Jones sprang from the floor and snatched the net. He aimed carefully and struck the snake square in the midsection. For the first time, the snake flinched. "The spot where I hit him was as big around as my calf. He started to uncoil, and at first I couldn't tell if he was coming in or going out. Luckily he went out."

The snake dropped into the water, and for the first time, Jones had a clear view of his body. He swung hard and fast with the net and struck the snake across the head. The snake went limp and sank beneath the surface.

"When he went limp," Jones said, "he straightened out

completely, and I said to Paul, 'My God, look at the size of him!' That snake was at least six feet long, and Paul told me he counted eight or nine buttons on his tail."

After the snake disappeared, Jones turned and looked at Shepherd in disbelief. When he turned back around, the snake was coming straight at them.

"It was like a nightmare," Jones said. "The rattlesnake had come back to life, and I knew then that he was after us. He swam to the side of the boat and started coming out of the water. That's when I lost it. I grabbed the net again and started flailing with everything I had. I must have hurt him, because he turned away, swam to the opposite side of the cove, and coiled up underneath a tree."

Jones and Shepherd moved farther away, finally free of the snake, but couldn't stop talking about it.

"We realized that all we had to do was start the big engine and drive away," Jones said. "But we were too panicked. Plus, we never imagined the snake would come after us in the first place."

Thirty minutes later the two anglers resumed fishing, and that night they were awarded the 15th-place check in the tournament.

"We really felt like we'd earned it," Jones said. "The fishing hadn't been very good, but we finished in the money. Now whenever I'm fishing, I carry a big stick. It can get real spooky out there once you've had a rattlesnake that big chase your boat and try to come in after you."

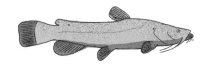

CATFISH ATTACK, NOW AND THEN

Way back in 1992, the *Indiana Telegraph* reported on a catfish story that I'd never thought was possible. Mitchell Franklin was fishing with friends at a local lake when he landed a 5-pound catfish. As a joke, he unhooked the fish and tossed it to his buddy, who quickly tossed it back. Franklin, however, wasn't expecting the return pitch. The catfish slammed into his chest, impaling him with its 5-inch poisonous spine. Paramedics were called and Franklin was rushed to St. Mary's Medical Center, where he underwent surgery to repair a collapsed lung. He remained hospitalized and on antibiotics to combat the effects of the toxins injected into his chest by the catfish spine.

Move ahead to 2013, when 13-year-old Aiden Menchaca was fishing with his family at a lake near Maumelle, Arkansas. Aiden caught a small catfish, and when his mother, Melissa Menchaca, held it up for Aiden to kiss before release, the fish flopped free and impaled young Aiden in the neck. The poisonous barb pierced his artery, causing the blood vessel to bulge out. Fearing catastro-

FISH FACT
Fish glue made from cod skin has been used as adhesive on stamps.

phe, Melissa held the fish in place as her husband called 911. Thirty minutes later, paramedics arrived and cut the base of the fin. They then rushed Aiden to Arkansas Children's Hospital, where doctors successfully removed the barb, which was only centimeters from Aiden's main artery.

The poisonous barb of the catfish runs along its back and is extremely effective as a defense from predators.

SEATED, 80 FEET BELOW SEA LEVEL

Paul Claus felt the water surrounding him and knew he would soon drown. The heavy chair he was strapped to was bolted to the engine cover and both were sinking fast. And 800 pounds of blue marlin towed all of it straight down.

It was November 1984, and Claus had hooked his first marlin. He and Glenn Van Valin, owner of the 26-foot fishing boat *Karma*, had fished together many times before. This was a day they would never forget.

"Bait had been easy to find," Claus said, "and by six thirty in the morning we were hooked up. The fish hit immediately, even before Glenn could get the line in the outrigger. I jumped into the chair and slipped into the harness. It was loose, but I never had a chance to tighten it. There was also a seat belt to keep me snug in the chair, and when the marlin got close, Glenn told me to unsnap it in case he needed my help. Unsnapping the belt and wearing a loose harness probably saved my life."

One end of a thick, ⅝-inch-diameter nylon rope was tied to the base of the fighting chair, the other end to the flying gaff. The fighting chair was fastened to the engine cover, and the engine cover to the deck. Stainless steel held everything in place. As Van Valin reached over the transom, preparing to gaff the fish, neither could have guessed what would happen next.

"The first thing I remember is the explosion of fish and water," Claus said. "Then I felt this tremendous jerk and I was flying through the air. I remember the panic as I tried to grab things on my way out of the boat—Glenn, the railing, anything to save my life."

Claus didn't know it then, but the marlin had ripped the 4-by-6-foot engine cover from its bolts, carrying it and the fighting chair overboard. "When I hit the water, I could see junk all around me. There was incredible chaos, and the pressure was enormous—not from the depth, but from the speed and the resistance of the water. It felt like a speedboat was pulling me headfirst under the water. I couldn't move.

"I thought I was going to die, and a lot of things went through my mind. Then I had this overpowering urge to fight. It was a stupid way to die, and I got mad. I started struggling to slide my arm under the harness. I remember getting it free and reaching up. Then everything stopped. There was no more chaos, no more pressure, just silence and darkness." Claus was near death. He could see hazy sunlight in one direction and darkness in the other. He surged toward the light. His lungs tore at his throat. His head throbbed. His vision began to narrow.

FISH FACT
Before sandpaper was invented, sharkskin was used.

His wife, Donna, who had been driving the boat, was hysterical. Van Valin, who had been struck by the chair and the engine cover, was dazed and bleeding. Both were in shock as they searched the water for signs of Claus.

"When I didn't think I could go any further," Claus said, "I looked up and saw the hull of the boat. It was a struggle to stay conscious, but somehow I made it. The first breath of air felt like a second chance at life. Glenn was all banged up, and Donna was crying. That's when I realized how lucky I'd been. They helped me up into the boat, but I couldn't stand. I found later that my inner ears were filled with water."

Van Valin had broken some ribs and needed 18 stitches to repair the wounds to his head. Claus had no visible injuries. Although the pressure of his descent had forced water through his ears, the eardrums were not damaged.

"A few days after the accident," Claus said, "I went back out with scuba gear to gauge my depth. I took my mask off underwater and looked up at the boat. I estimated my deepest point at eighty feet, and thirty feet when I first saw the hull of the boat.

"Donna told me later that I had been underwater for more than a minute and a half. A few more seconds and I never would have made it."

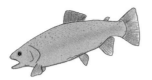

A NOSE FOR TROUT

ortunately, Bill Poyneer's rainbow trout was a trophy-size fish. Otherwise, his unpleasant experience on Mexican Hay Lake would have remained just that.

The balmy summer morning was clear when Poyneer paddled his canoe to the center of the lake, one of many sprinkled across the Indian reservations of Arizona's White Mountains. He carried a fly rod, a tackle box, and a 12-gauge shotgun in his canoe. When the fishing slowed, he planned to hunt ducks.

"Mexican Hay is shallow," Poyneer said, "only about four feet deep all the way across. I was fishing the middle of the lake when I saw a waterspout over on one side. It hit a boat and flipped it over. Summer was the time of year for the little whirlwinds of sand called dust devils, and when they crossed the water they created waterspouts. I knew this one was traveling my way, but I thought it would miss me."

Once he saw that it was coming right at him, Poyneer paddled frantically. But the waterspout was too swift. It caught Poyneer and capsized his canoe. Poyneer retrieved his gear from the lake's shallow bottom, righted his canoe, and returned to shore. "That should have been a warning," he said. "But it was early in the day and

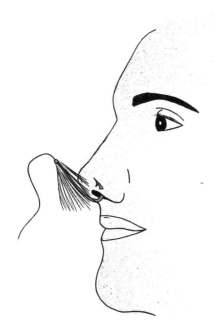

I wanted to fly-fish." He dried his gun, changed into dry clothes, and laid his wet clothes in the sun. Then he gathered up his fly gear and returned to the lake in a float tube.

"I hooked a big trout on my three-weight rod," Poyneer said, "and played it for about twenty minutes. It came up a few feet away from the float tube and lay on its side. I thought it was dead."

Since he had no net, Poyneer lifted the fly rod high and pulled the trout toward the float tube. The trout was heavy, and the fly rod strained against the weight. When it was just within Poyneer's reach, the fish came to life suddenly and leaped. The fly came unhooked and snapped back at Poyneer's face. The airborne fish landed inside the float tube and flopped wildly about. Blood spilled down Poyneer's face.

"It was awful," Poyneer said. "The fly went right up my nose, and it was the first time all day that I hadn't pinched down the barb on the hook. I knew I couldn't get the fly out, so I cut the line and kicked back to shore. The trout was dead in the tube and there was blood everywhere."

Poyneer drove 35 minutes to the nearest hospital, where the fly was surgically removed from his nostril. "All the nurses and doctors came to see the fisherman with a fly up his nose," he said. "It caused a lot of interest."

Two stitches later and hours after getting hooked, he returned to the lake. "I didn't get back there until late that afternoon. By then I had to pack up and head home."

FISH FACT
A hagfish will bore a hole in its prey and eat it from the inside out until there is nothing left but skin and bones.

The rainbow trout measured 25 inches from nose to tail and weighed 5 pounds. It was the largest and most memorable rainbow trout Poyneer has yet caught. Today, the notorious fish is displayed proudly on a wall at Tight Lines, Poyneer's fly-fishing shop in Tucson, Arizona.

Is there a gleam of revenge in that fish eye?

CLASSIC

WAHOO ATTACK

Lou Wiczai took his position at the stern of the 92-foot charter fishing boat *Royal Star*. He was one of more than 30 anglers deep in wahoo country, 500 miles south of Cabo San Lucas, Mexico. The island of Roca Partida, the first stop of their 16-day trip, rose solemnly in the distance, marking the location of some of the best game-fishing water in the world.

Wiczai, a burly veteran and unflagging tuna fisherman, waited with three other anglers for the signal from skipper Dave Kagawa to toss out the first lures of the trip. Kagawa had divided the anglers into teams of four, each angler trolling from the stern in half-hour increments. When the signal was given, Wiczai positioned his lure beyond the wake, and his rod jerked forward with a strike. It was the first fish of the trip.

After adding another wahoo and a small tuna to his sack, Wiczai was back in position trolling from the stern. This time the angler at the starboard corner was first to hook up. The boat stopped and the waiting anglers rushed the bait wells, anticipating game fish below.

FISH FACT
The word *angler* is Old English for "hook."

Wiczai wound in his lure and lifted it from the

surface. As he turned his back to change fishing rods, he glimpsed a flurry of splashes off the stern and a shadow coming toward him. Instinctively, he raised his arm to cover his face.

Mouth agape, a 40-pound wahoo smashed into his forearm. The force of the blow slammed his arm against his head, shattering his glasses. The wahoo ricocheted off, splashed back into the sea, and swam away.

"I looked at my arm, and all I saw was blood," Wiczai said. "My first thought was, 'Oh God, there goes my fishing trip!'"

The wahoo, which had vaulted from the sea in pursuit of an angler's lure, had ripped its teeth into the top of Wiczai's forearm. Blood gushed from the deep 3-inch gash, leaving delicate arteries exposed.

The skipper and crew rushed to Wiczai's aid, cleaning and packing the wound with fresh gauze. Within minutes, they were headed toward Socorro Island, the largest island in the Revillagigedo chain and site of the only medical facility within 500 miles.

The skipper radioed ahead with the emergency report. The control responded: the doctor would meet them at Socorro. Meanwhile, Leroy Shintaku, the second skipper aboard, radioed the U.S. Coast Guard. The coast guard responded with an emergency plane en route from San Diego.

Later, his arm bandaged and held high above his head, Wiczai arrived at Socorro. The doctor repacked his arm with fresh gauze, injected him with antibiotics, and recommended a trip to a major hospital. Wiczai was taken to the island's airport—a bare strip of land and an aged macadam airstrip covered with cracks, weeds, and occasional herds of wild goats. No lights illuminated the runway, and no control tower regulated the random flights.

The coast guard plane arrived at dusk, and as it came to a stop, the hatchway opened and two medics exited, expecting a broken-down old man. Instead they found Wiczai, a tough ex-sailor who wanted only to return to fishing.

"I'd never caused such a fuss in all my life," Wiczai said. "I knew I was injured, but I felt just fine."

After a quick checkup, the medics put him on the plane and he was flown to San Diego. Nerves in his arm were damaged, and the wound was open to infection. Surgery was required. A naval ambulance was waiting in San Diego when Wiczai arrived, to take him to San Diego Naval Hospital. It was 10 p.m., 15 hours since his injury. Wiczai underwent surgery and spent five days in the hospital recovering from his injury.

Although he lost partial use of his hand, his fishing was not affected. "I owe a lot of thanks to everyone involved," Wiczai said. "Without them, I probably wouldn't be here planning my next fishing trip."

FRESHWATER CROCODILES

C olin Cordingly, three-time winner of the prestigious Barramundi Classic, is one of the best-known barramundi fishermen in Australia. But with the fame comes the risk of attack by Australia's notorious freshwater crocodiles.

"If you fish barramundi," Cordingly said, "you learn to live with the crocs."

One of Cordingly's most harrowing experiences took place on the Finniss River on the west side of the Northern Territory at a water hole called Sweet's Lookout.

"It's a well-known barramundi spot," Cordingly said. "'Sweet' stands for Sweetheart, an eighteen-foot crocodile who used to live there. Sweetheart never attacked any anglers, but engine noises upset her."

Cordingly and his friends were fishing from two 12-foot aluminum boats. As his friends rounded a bend in the river, Sweetheart emerged from the water and attacked their outboard motor. She shook the small craft in her jaws and snapped the motor in half. Then she grabbed the boat by the transom and began tearing it to pieces.

"One of my mates picked up an oar," Cordingly recalled, "and hit Sweetheart in the head. This made her even angrier, and she ripped the oar from his hands. My other mate was at the bow, paddling like mad to get away. As Sweetheart chewed on the oar, they came back around the bend so fast they were nearly planing the boat. Some other fishermen were close by, and they came to their rescue and towed their damaged boat to safety."

Cordingly had had another frightening incident that took place years earlier during an excursion on the East Alligator River.

"The river was at about half-tide," he said, "and we were traveling at full planing speed up one of the many small creeks that flow into the outback. In this creek, the tidal water had dropped so low that its banks were about four or five feet above our heads."

Cordingly was standing at the wheel of the small outboard boat when he felt a gust of wind brush across the top of his head. He turned toward the bank and saw dirt tumbling into the creek. Then he heard a splash on the opposite side of the boat.

"The creek was only seven or eight feet wide," Cordingly said, "so at first I thought the falling dirt was caused by the wash from our boat. But one of my blokes was

FISH FACT
Certain jellyfish travel by wind power and can alter the curve of their sails depending on the direction of the wind.

sitting in the bow facing me, and when I saw his eyes all buggered out I knew something must have happened."

Earlier that day, during high tide, an 18-foot crocodile had crawled onto the bank to sun himself and had lain there asleep until Cordingly's engine startled him. The groggy crocodile had lunged for the safety of the water just as the boat drove by, missing Cordingly's head by inches.

"I never saw him," Cordingly said. "But if the bank of the creek had given way a little more, two tons of angry crocodile would have landed right in our boat."

This is not the sort of guest you want to come upon unexpectedly.

SNAKE BIT

Certain southern swamplands hold record numbers of large-mouth bass. They also hold deadly water moccasins.

Cecil Conners was fishing a favorite Louisiana location, when he landed a fat 3-pound bass. Conners happily raised the fish and reached into its wide mouth to remove the hook. A searing pain caused him to drop the bass and grab his injured hand. Moments later, Conners spotted the cause of the intense pain. A water moccasin, which the bass had ingested minutes earlier, was wriggling free of the bass's maw. Conners was rushed to the hospital, where he was treated for a most unusual catch and release.

FISH FACT
The poison from a Portuguese man of war is 75 times more potent than cobra venom.

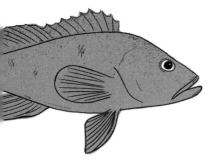

POP GOES THE DINGHY

R ob Cassady and Bill Hannah hauled the rubber dinghy down the beach to the shore of El Embarco Dorado, Mexico, a small uncharted location on the southern Sea of Cortez. They loaded their fishing gear, jumped inside, and zoomed out to sea. It was October, the peak of the fishing season at the East Cape.

They slowed at the local wahoo grounds, a mile or so from shore, and tossed out two shiny jet-head jigs—a favorite wahoo snack. Cassady sat at the stern, holding the throttle in one hand and his fishing rod in the other. After a few passes across the grounds, a huge shadow appeared behind Cassady's jig. Seconds later, the surface exploded—*Wham! Wham! Wham!*—with the bill of a small blue marlin.

"It was incredible," Cassady said. "We never expected a marlin to be so close to shore, and we especially never thought one would hit my tiny wahoo jig."

The marlin turned and zoomed across the surface, jumping more than 20 times before finally sounding into the warm currents of the Sea of Cortez, hauling the boat behind it. Cassady clung to the fishing rod. He had no rod belt to cushion the rod butt, which ground painfully into his gut. The dinghy was cramped and wobbly

and offered no protection from the sun.

An hour passed. The marlin surfaced again and was tiring. Cassady fought steadily, gaining line with each turn of the spool. Soon the anglers were within reach of the leader and could see the lavender hue of the fish beneath the boat.

"It was eerie," Cassady said. "The marlin seemed to look right into my eyes. I got scared for the first time and realized how vulnerable we were. We were five or six miles from shore, and the wind was picking up. The sea was getting rough and every wave felt big."

But there was no time for fear. The marlin dashed away, stripping line from the reel. Cassady leaned against the weight with aching muscles. It seemed hopeless to try to land a marlin from such a flimsy boat. Fuel, weather, and especially drinking water were mounting concerns. Then the line went slack. He reeled frantically, hoping the marlin had only changed course. Suddenly the surface erupted in a spray of water. It was the marlin, still hooked and heading straight for the dinghy.

"His tail was all we could see," Cassady said. "It was moving so fast that it looked like the spray from a motorboat. I knew we were in trouble and yelled for Bill to watch out."

The marlin charged. Cassady and Hannah ducked. Huddled together, they covered their heads with their arms, expecting the marlin to leap over the dinghy. But the marlin never left the water.

"When I felt the impact," Cassady said, "I didn't know what to expect. I looked up and saw the marlin thrashing around. His bill was stuck in the side of the dinghy and he couldn't get free. We were taking on a lot of water and losing air fast."

Hannah reached out and gripped the marlin by the bill, gaffing him in the flank with a small hand gaff. The marlin bucked and shook the dinghy violently. Cassady scrambled for an oar and, in a desperate attempt to save their lives, began beating the marlin over the head.

"I was totally panicked," Cassady said. "We were miles from shore and I'd seen a lot of sharks around. It was life or death as far as I was concerned."

The marlin stopped thrashing, and Cassady laid down the oar. Air rushed from the gash in the side of the dinghy. Hannah stuffed his fingers into the hole. They slid the marlin into the boat and steered for shore.

The rubber gunwale was just above water level when the dinghy streaked into the bay and onto the beach. A crowd of campers gathered around them. The fish was hauled to a nearby tree and hung from a limb for photographs. The catch, a small blue marlin, was estimated to weigh 150 pounds.

"To me it seemed like the biggest marlin in the world," Cassady said.

CRASHING BLACK MARLIN

It's not every day that a big billfish crashes over the gunwale of a sportfisher and flings furniture at its pursuers. But that's exactly what happened on a rough day outside Cairns, Australia. The captain of the *Little Audrey* was backing down on an estimated 600-pound black marlin while his angler reeled frantically to keep the fishing line taut. Soon the fish was within tagging range, when it turned and slashed its enormous tail and leaped from the water, soaring halfway into the cockpit. The marlin balanced on the rail, slashing its huge bill before sliding back into the sea, still hooked. After a few minutes of pandemonium, and only minor injuries, the behemoth was released unharmed.

> **FISH FACT**
> The first thing a sea horse does after being born is swim to the surface and gulp air to fill its swim bladder.

This incredible fishing moment was captured on video (follow the links at shaunmorey.com).

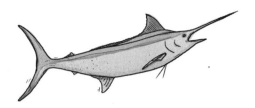

CAUGHT BELOW THE BELT

I met Captain Laurie Woodbridge on the deck of his 40-foot sportfisher, *Sea Baby II*, in Cairns, Australia, in May 1989. It was off-season, and the wharf was peaceful and quiet.

We talked about his unbeaten 1,347-pound world record—a black marlin caught by angler Morton May on 80-pound test. He told me of the year he captured 15 granders, weighing in 9. That was the same year a 1,287-pound black marlin speared his boat, drilling a hole through the lower transom. As the boat began to sink, Woodbridge's deckie shoved a broom handle into the hole. They saved the boat—and landed the fish.

But Woodbridge's favorite story is the one about the novice angler from America whose first fight with a large black marlin nearly cost him his manhood.

"Our angler was an American bloke who'd never caught a big fish in his life and didn't know what to expect. We were in the familiar areas, looking for his first marlin, when the port rigger snapped and our fish was on. Sitting in the fighting chair, harnessed and all clipped in, the angler was watching the marlin jump across the water when it changed course and came toward the boat.

"The fish had slowed down and was underwater, so I backed

the boat up very gently to let the angler get a closer look at him. Leaning forward, the angler grabbed the foregrip of the rod and began to angle it like a light-tackle fisherman. Nobody saw him do it, and the harness began to slip up from under his bum and work its way up and across the top of his back.

"The leader was almost out of the water when the angler jerked the rod a couple of times, spooking the fish. Keep in mind that the rod is locked into the gimbal on the chair between the angler's legs, and the harness, which is now well up his back, is locked to the reel, causing him to crouch over the rod. The fish took off, racing toward the horizon. There were forty-five pounds of strike drag on the line, and the fisherman wasn't ready for it when it came right.

"Things happened rather quickly. The rod jerked forward and slammed down over the transom railing, and the angler, with his hand wrapped around the foregrip, followed, letting out a scream as his feet came off the footrest of the chair.

"One second he was sitting up, the next he was lying horizontal across the top of the rod, parallel to the deck and straddling the reel, his hands flailing in the air as he tried to regain his balance.

"The fish was ripping the line off the reel at a blistering pace, and the angler, wearing nothing but his underpants because of the heat that day, lay helplessly over the scorching reel. The spinning line quickly burned through the fork of his pants, and we heard another chilling scream.

"The crewman tried desperately to get the reel to release the drag, but the angler had it covered completely with his body. Luckily the fish stopped its run, and the angler was pushed back into the chair. A detailed check of his anatomy followed, revealing some painful marks but no real damage.

FISH FACT

Halibut, like all flatfish, are born looking like typical fish. As they mature, they flatten and their eyes shift to one side of their body. If the eyes are on the right side, it's a halibut. If the eyes are on the left, it's a turbot.

"We settled down to a lengthy fight and finally managed to tag and release the eight-hundred-pound marlin—a catch that angler will surely never forget."

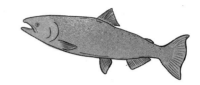

37 HOURS ON ROD AND REEL

It was just after noon on July 12, 1989. Bob Ploeger, his wife, Darlean, and fishing guide Dan Bishop sat in the drift boat floating down Alaska's Kenai River. They were enjoying their first trip to Alaska and their first time salmon fishing. Half a day of fishing was all they had planned. Two days later, exhausted and bewildered, they would wonder what had happened.

"We'd fished all morning," Ploeger explained, "and I hadn't had a strike. Darlean had hooked a couple of small fish, but that was all. At about noon, Dan Bishop rowed us out into the center of the river and anchored the boat so that he could eat lunch.

"Darlean and I kept fishing, and about the time Dan finished his sandwich I had a hit. It was the hardest hit I'd ever felt. I pulled back hard and set the hook, and for the next two hours I fought the fish from the anchored boat. Then the fish took off out of its hole and went downstream as fast as he could go. Dan pulled up the anchor, lifted the paddles, and began rowing in pursuit."

It was a frantic run for the three anglers. The salmon was swimming downcurrent faster than Bishop could paddle. Line kept spinning from the reel. The fish wasn't tiring, and Ploeger watched helplessly as the thin metal spool began to show beneath the 30-pound monofilament. Desperate to stop the fish, he pressed his thumb down over the line. The fish slowed, turned, and swam back upstream.

"We were relieved to have turned the fish," Ploeger said, "until we saw the island in the middle of the river. The fish was going up the opposite side of it and against the current. Bishop tried to follow, but the current was too strong. I was sure we'd lose the fish."

Suddenly the line stopped flowing from the reel. Once around the island, the salmon had paused to rest in some rapids. Relieved, Bishop paddled to the island and flagged down a motorized skiff. He and Ploeger quickly switched boats and drove upriver to the rapids. After a few tugs on the line, the salmon darted away from the rapids, turning back the way it had come. Darlean remained on the island with the owners of the motorized skiff and later returned to camp.

Four hours into the fight, Ploeger's fish had moved more than a mile downriver and was across from the docks where the day of fishing had begun. It was there, after sulking in the mud for 30 minutes, that the salmon first jumped. It was a giant fish, the largest salmon any of them had ever seen.

The salmon was strong and stubborn, staying on the bottom and downcurrent through most of the fight—the first part of which went on for 30 hours. Ploeger kept pressure on the line and remained patient.

FISH FACT

Sea lions have ears and swim with their foreflippers; seals lack external ears and swim with their hind flippers.

During the first night, Ploeger and Bishop switched to a third boat with greater fuel capacity. A crowd had gathered along the shore of the Kenai, and many of the local charter captains were congregating on the river offering their assistance.

Also during the night, media began to arrive with camera equipment and more boats. Reporters and photographers were allowed on board to interview Ploeger and record his battle with the mammoth salmon. At 10:30 p.m., the fish surfaced once more, then settled back in the mud. The night dragged on. The guides slept in rotation while Ploeger waited for daybreak.

By dawn, nothing had changed. The river was only 8 feet deep, so Bishop tried stabbing an oar into the shallow riverbed, attempting to scare the fish, but to no avail. Between 5:00 that morning and 8:00 that night, the fish had moved only 100 yards.

By this time, local radio stations had arrived and set up remote broadcasting from the shoreline. Many more spectators had also arrived, swelling the banks of the Kenai to capacity. At 8:30 p.m., a radio station announced over loudspeakers that Ploeger had broken the Guinness world record for the longest fight on rod and reel—32 hours and 5 minutes. The onlookers cheered their approval.

Five more hours passed before the fish made its final run. It darted toward shore, and the camera crew, still aboard, shone their lights into the water. The fish was exhausted. Hovering a few feet beneath the water, it approached the river's edge.

The banks of the Kenai are steep and the water only a few feet deep. The salmon hit the steep edge and stopped. Bishop yelled for Ploeger to yank back to try to raise the fish, but the salmon didn't move.

Bishop made a difficult decision. It would be risky to try to scoop the fish from the bottom, but an even greater risk to miss the opportunity to capture the cornered fish. Ploeger had been fighting for more than 37 hours and was beyond exhaustion. The reel's gear was wearing, and the hook could work free any moment.

Bishop and another guide each handled a net—one 3 feet in diameter, the other 4 feet. They corralled the fish, boxing it in, sensing victory.

The water swirled along the shore when one of the nets brushed Ploeger's leader. The line broke, the rod snapped back, and the plug fell from the salmon's mouth.

Both guides fought desperately to scoop the salmon into the nets. But the river bottom was covered with rocks, and each time they pushed, the nets snagged and the boat slid farther away. Suddenly, the current caught the fish and swept it around the nets and into the murky water.

Ploeger stood in the boat, staring helplessly into the river. The fish he had worked so hard for was free. The guides threw their nets down in disgust, and the camera crew shut off the lights. The battle was over. The salmon had won.

CLASSIC GIANT CATFISH CHOKEHOLD

Only one thing interests John Pidcock when he fishes. Catfish. Large catfish. Catfish that lurk in dark, dangerous crevices. Catfish the size of pickle barrels.

Pidcock scouts the rivers of central Oklahoma for beaver dens, overhanging banks, large boulders, and deepwater holes—the probable places where catfish nest and spawn. He carries no fishing gear, just a waterskiing rope for a stringer. He noodles. He swims into a murky catfish hole, gropes about for the smooth, motionless fish, and attempts to provoke it to bite him. When the catfish attacks, Pidcock reaches into the fish's open mouth and pulls it out by hand. This practice, called noodling, is legal—and popular—in many southern states.

"We start in the spring," Pidcock explained, "just as soon as the water warms up enough so you can get in."

Noodling is not without risks, and Pidcock understands them well: beaver bites, poisonous snakes, jagged rocks, and some catfish so large they can hold a man down. "There was an old man who noodled over in Chicken Creek near Tenkiller Lake," Pidcock said. "He caught several fish ninety pounds and bigger back in the 1920s. One of those big flatheads bit him up past his elbow and raked all the meat off his forearm. They had to amputate his arm."

Pidcock retains his limbs, but two seasons ago, while feeling for a large catfish in a deserted beaver den on Cimarron River, he was bitten on the hand by a startled muskrat. Pidcock, who plays guitar at a local club and noodles with gloves to protect his hands, had reached into the air pocket where the muskrat lived. The muskrat clamped its jaws around his fingers, sending a sudden numbing sensation up his hand.

Pidcock returned to the river's edge and removed the bloodied glove. The top of the glove had been pierced, but there were no holes in the bottom. One of his fingers, however, had been bitten clean through. "The bottom teeth must have missed," Pidcock said, "but the top teeth went all the way through, just missing the bone."

In July 1993, in the Deep Fork River, Pidcock noodled his largest catfish. He had squirmed far back into a beaver's den and cornered the fish. When it bit him, he reached into its mouth with both hands and grasped it by its thick, toothy lower lip. Two of Pidcock's friends, Carl Harris and Ivan Church, stood at the entrance to the den and held his legs. Pidcock signaled and his friends yanked him from the hole. The catfish emerged last, clamped to Pidcock's hands.

FISH FACT
Narwhals have no fins, and the tusk protruding as long as 9 feet from its head is actually one of its two teeth.

"That catfish weighed forty-eight pounds," Pidcock said, "and its bottom jaw was as big around as a piece of luggage. When it clamped down on my hand, it bit so hard it broke one of my fingers."

Noodlers target catfish during spawning season, when the usually docile fish become aggressive and are enticed to bite. They look forward all winter to the day when they can shimmy through the basketball-size tunnels that lead from the riverbank into large underground beaver dens where the large catfish lie, waiting to spawn and quick to attack.

"There's nothing more gratifying than getting bit by a big catfish," Pidcock said. "The adrenaline rush is unbelievable."

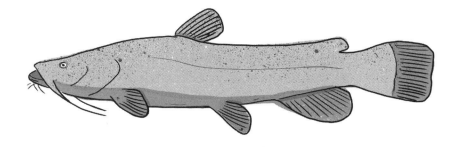

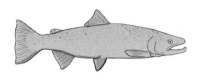

ORCA HOOKUP

It was early January when Bert Swift left the dock aboard his 26-foot sportfisher *Tolly* and headed to the south end of Vashon Island in Puget Sound, Washington, for a day of winter steelhead fishing—known locally as blackmouth fishing. The tide would change at noon, so by 10:30 he had set his downrigger to 150 feet and began to troll his favorite white squid-shaped jig and glowing foot-long flasher.

"The first hit was a gentle tap," Swift said, "then a few more followed, but nothing stuck. I lowered the downrigger to two hundred and fifty feet, and around one in the afternoon, after the tide had changed, I got a hard strike."

Swift rushed to the controls and stopped the boat, and then hurried back to the stern to fight the fish. Within minutes, the fish had made two long, deep runs.

"I was excited by its size and thought maybe it was close to the thirty-three-pounder caught recently off Jefferson Head."

Ten more minutes passed and the fish was still going strong. More than 200 feet of fishing line was off of the reel and the fish was still taking line.

"I knew it was a big fish, when all of a sudden the line went slack. I cranked the reel and still nothing. All I could think of was that the fish was swimming right toward the boat. Then I felt a tug, followed by a second tug, and then a third."

Fifty feet from the back of Swift's boat appeared the tip of a slick black fin. Slowly it grew in size until it was 4 feet above the surface. The fin was followed by a massive curved back that released a whoosh of air that whistled across the water. Orca!

"I was mesmerized by the beauty and size of the whale, but I made sure I continued to crank on the fishing line. Suddenly, the orca popped its head above the water and I spotted the tail of my fish sticking out of its mouth with my foot-long flasher dangling alongside! I couldn't believe it. I had actually caught an orca whale!"

The whale, unperturbed by the flasher or the fishing line, shook its head and sank beneath the surface.

"My reel took off and all I could do was thumb the spool and hope my seventeen-pound line would hold."

Seconds later, the sound of the fishing line snapping was like a gun going off in the quiet afternoon.

"I can't explain whether I was disappointed or angry or just plain excited. I'd lost a lot of gear and the largest steelhead salmon I'd ever hooked, but soon after that, I spotted the entire pod of killer whales.

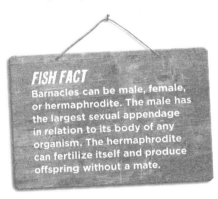

FISH FACT
Barnacles can be male, female, or hermaphrodite. The male has the largest sexual appendage in relation to its body of any organism. The hermaphrodite can fertilize itself and produce offspring without a mate.

There were nine orcas, three of which were huge males over twenty-five feet long. I also saw two calves. The orcas hung around and put on quite a show. And on my way back to the dock, I was accompanied by three of the orcas. They stayed within twenty yards of me and jumped a few times as if to say thanks for the fish. I know I felt the same way."

It was one of the few (known) times a sea mammal as intelligent as an orca had taken a hooked fish from an angler. The pod seemed especially curious and playful, and it is possible that the orca took the opportunity of an easy catch to teach a younger killer whale how to eat a salmon. The pod may also have been a local family familiar with powerboats, which may explain their lack of wariness and willingness to steal the fish and then hang around to play.

TARPON BODY SLAM

Fishing a few hundred yards off the shores of Cape Canaveral, Florida, David and Marc Rocque hooked a huge tarpon from their small 22-foot boat. During the fight, the tarpon closed in on the boat and leaped inside, knocking David overboard. David sputtered to the surface, holding his fishing rod. He swam back to the boat and held on as the tarpon tired. Buckets of bait had been chummed to attract the tarpon—and there was a large shark that the brothers had seen earlier, circling the boat.

FISH FACT
The largest fish caught from shore was a 1,780-pound tiger shark caught from a jetty in South Carolina.

Once David was back aboard, the brothers landed and released the fish. Then they inspected the boat. Not only had the tarpon crashed into David, but it had also managed to break numerous fishing rods, a downrigger boom, and the outboard engine before it flopped back out of the boat.

DR. FISHHOOK

CLASSIC

D r. Nils Olson knows more about fishhooks than most anyone on the planet. Not because he designs them or pins bait onto them or pitches them for rising game fish. Dr. Olson knows about fishhooks because he specializes in removing them from people.

"I started in fishhook removal in 1974," the doctor said, "but it wasn't until the early nineties that it really took off. The O. J. Simpson trial was going on, and I think the media was looking for a diversion. Our local television station did an interview about how many fishermen were getting stuck by fishhooks."

Soon, Dr. Olson's expertise in fishhook removal was written up on the front page of the Milwaukee *Journal Sentinel* newspaper. Then it spread to the Chicago newspapers and eventually to NBC. "The television reporter did a story on me," Olson explained, "and soon anyone within a hundred miles of my clinic was coming in with imbedded fishhooks."

Over the years, Dr. Olson has seen fish-hooks buried in the backs of heads, hands, arms, faces, and even lips. "The only place

FISH FACT
Stingray tails inject poison into predators and unsuspecting humans, and also cut the flesh of prey for easy consumption.

I haven't removed a fishhook from is a tongue," he explained. "I guess it's just a matter of time."

One of the perks of being the country's leading fishhook remover is the collection of lures he has on his trophy wall. Anglers are often so happy to have the hook out of their skin that they gladly donate the hardware to the doctor, who hangs them from a board in his office. "I have so many now," he said, "more than I ever thought was possible. Beautiful lures of every shape and size."

And each lure has a story. "One of the funniest ones was a patient who came in with the lure caught in his lips and the packaging still attached. He'd been in the hardware store and must have been trying to open the lure with his teeth when he got hooked.

"Another time, this young man came in with a spear through his hand. It's illegal to spearfish in Wisconsin, but people do it. This man dropped the spear, and as he went to grab for it, the point went right through his palm—all the way through, with the barb out the other side. I had to drive to the hardware store and buy a pair of heavy-duty bolt cutters to snip off the end of the spear, so I could free it before sewing up the wound.

"But my all-time favorite was the day a local muskie guide came in with a big lure hooked arm and arm to his client. He swore me to secrecy so I can't tell you his name, but that big muskie lure with its forward and trailing razor-sharp treble hooks had them both snagged in tandem."

SKEWERED IN AUSTRALIA

Two of Australia's most revered big-game skippers, Captain Peter Wright of the sportfisher *Kingfish* and Captain Peter Bristow aboard the *Avalon*, left their home port of Cairns, Australia, and headed north toward Lizard Island, a little-known island near the tip of the Great Barrier Reef. Few had fished these far-off waters, but those who had, like legendary angler Bob Dyer, returned with tales of extraordinary catches and epic battles.

"The marlin fishing in this area, which was rarely fished, was phenomenal," Wright said. "We made our way farther and farther north, never sure if we were still on the marlin grounds. We might have a slow day, but then we'd have a really hot day and knew we hadn't gone too far."

It was late September 1972, and the boats had just finished a run at the top end of Ribbon Reef Number 10. Bill Chapman, who had caught more 1,000-pound marlin than any other angler at that time, was Wright's angler for the trip. They'd just left the reef and were entering an area known as Cormorant Pass, when the starboard reel hissed with a strike. Within moments, 600 solid pounds of black marlin took to the sky.

"I could see that the wire leader was wrapped," Wright said, "so I turned and chased the fish and quickly got right up on him. Bill was reeling fast and got most of the line back on, when I spun the boat and began backing down on him. The fish was tailing down sea, and with Bill pulling hard and me backing down, we were able to overtake the fish while he was still plenty fresh."

Mutt Coble, one of the deckhands aboard, grabbed the leader, while the other deckhand, Jimmy Byrnes, reached out with the tagging stick. The marlin, still twisted in the wire leader, jumped and landed awkwardly on its back. Byrnes leaned over the transom for another attempt to tag the fish before release, but the marlin surged upward, and before Wright could gun the throttles, the airborne marlin speared Byrnes through the chest.

"I saw the marlin preparing for that second jump," Wright explained, "and I hit the throttles hard, but it happened too fast. I didn't know Jimmy had been hit. My worry was that Mutt's hands were wrapped in the wire leader. I yelled out for him when I heard him yell something about 'Got it!' I thought he meant Jimmy had tagged the fish."

FISH FACT
The swell shark not only expands itself into a balloon to ward off predators, but it also lays rectangular eggs.

As Mutt snapped the wire leader releasing the marlin, Wright put the boat into neutral and raced down to the cockpit to check on his team. "Jim was sitting on the deck," he said, "leaning against one of the seats with his hands over his chest. Blood was draining between his fingers."

Wright ripped open Byrnes's shirt, and was relieved to see only a small wound. Then he noticed the odd tissue hanging from the wound. Byrnes's lung had been punctured and the serrated marlin bill had pulled part of it out. A makeshift bandage was quickly applied to the wound while Wright hurried to radio for help.

"I had never been to that part of the reef before, but I knew there was a small landing strip on Lizard Island. Luckily I was able to alert the Royal Flying Doctor Service, and they agreed to send medical personnel to Lizard Island. I went back down to give the good news to Jim and check on his injury. I took off the bandage, and when he leaned forward a pool of blood spilled out. I knew right then how seriously he was hurt, and that if we didn't get him to a doctor soon he could bleed to death."

The pilot of the Royal Flying Doctors radioed that they were en route and would be at the island when the boat arrived. Wright was unfamiliar with the best approach to the island and was prepared to run aground if need be, when he spotted a commercial vessel. He radioed his need for a skiff to get his injured deckhand ashore.

"The commercial guys had a dory and let me use it to transport Jim to the island. There was a caretaker living in a tent who agreed to run us up in his tractor to the airstrip, where a doctor and a nurse were waiting. They had three large wooden boxes filled with medical equipment. They told me they'd brought everything they needed to perform open-heart surgery."

It had been 2 hours since the accident, and Byrnes was alive and stable enough for the flight back to the hospital in Cairns. The doctor, however, was worried about decompressing the wound at altitude, so the pilot flew dangerously low to the water, at 50 feet maximum, for the entire flight.

"It was about an hour later when they radioed back. Jim was in intensive care, but he would survive. We found out later that the marlin also broke three of his ribs. Three weeks later, though, he was back out on the boat, helping clients catch marlin, like he was born to do."

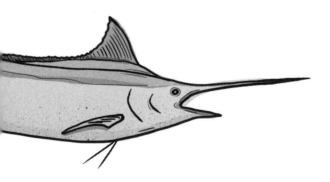

THE OUTRAGEOUS, THE CURIOUS, AND THE MERELY ODD

BLUE-RIBBON BLUEFINS

Captain Ed Murray with his crew and just two of the many giant bluefin tuna they've caught over the years

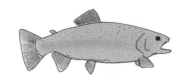

THUMBING FOR TROUT

Robert Lindsey sat at the bow of the ski boat, watching his young daughter busily playing at the stern. It was an ideal summer day, and Lindsey and a group of friends were boating on the Flaming Gorge Reservoir, a world-class trout destination that meanders along the Wyoming-Utah state line.

The midday boat ride had been pleasant and uneventful. Suddenly, the slow wake of a distant houseboat welled up and crashed over the ski boat's bow. The wall of water careened into Lindsey, knocking him off balance.

"All I remember is the wave coming over the boat," Lindsey said. "It went right over my back and filled the boat with water. One of my friend's daughters was sitting up front with me, and she was covered with water. Her mother was screaming, and as I regained my balance and bent down to help the girl, another wave came over the bow and threw me over the side."

The boat traveled over Lindsey, pinning him beneath the hull. He was upside down and moving headfirst toward the spinning propeller. His eyes were open, and he saw the bottom of the boat passing overhead.

"I knew I had to get out of here," Lindsey said. "I was trying to

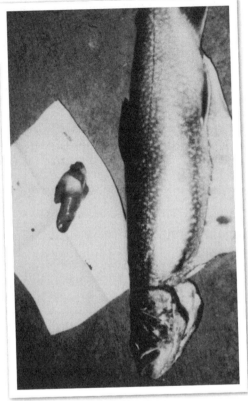
The gutted mackinaw trout and Robert Lindsey's severed thumb found inside the fish's belly

swim out from under the boat when I felt my hand go through the propeller. It's hard to explain the feeling. I didn't feel any pain, but I knew immediately that my hand was in bad shape."

Lindsey kicked hard to distance himself from the boat, but the twirling propeller caught his right leg and tore a deep gash from his knee to his foot. Moments later, dazed and bloodied, he surfaced.

"The first thing I saw was my index finger and my middle finger lying alongside my wrist," Lindsey said. "The only thing holding them on was a little piece of skin. Blood was squirting everywhere, and I couldn't see my thumb."

The boat had partially sunk and all the passengers were in the water. The children were accounted for while Lindsey treaded water nearby. He was without a life jacket and in shock.

"I was losing a lot of blood," Lindsey said, "and I was beginning to feel pretty weak. Finally, one of the guys swam over to help me. I latched on to his life jacket with my good hand and held on.

"There was a boat off in the distance, and we started yelling and hollering as loud as we could. I wanted out of the water real bad, and when the boat pulled up next to us I yanked myself out of the water with my one good hand."

Lindsey spent 17 days in the hospital and underwent reconstructive surgery to attach his two severed fingers. His thumb was gone, and his leg required numerous staples and stitches to repair the jagged wound.

Seven months after the accident, Lindsey's wife was told of a local newspaper article recounting a story about an angler who had discovered a human thumb in the belly of a trout. Blake Robinson had been ice fishing on the Flaming Gorge Reservoir when, late in the afternoon, he landed a 6-pound mackinaw trout. The fish was a keeper, measuring just under the 26- to 36-inch limit set by the state to protect the lake's trout population. Robinson stopped fishing and immediately filleted the trout on the frozen lake.

"When I cleaned the fish," he said, "I noticed that the belly looked like it had something in it. We'd been fishing with bullheads all day, and we wanted to see what else the fish had been eating. I cut open the trout's belly and out fell the thumb. At first it didn't register that it was a human thumb."

The thumb was well preserved,

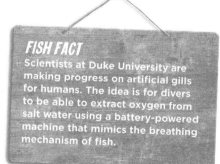

FISH FACT

Scientists at Duke University are making progress on artificial gills for humans. The idea is for divers to be able to extract oxygen from salt water using a battery-powered machine that mimics the breathing mechanism of fish.

and after recovering from the initial shock, Robinson wrapped it in a piece of cellophane. He marked the location on the ice with a red flag and took the thumb to the local sheriff's office. The sheriff filed a report and delivered the thumb to the local coroner, who placed it in a cooler.

"After reading the newspaper article," Lindsey said, "I called the coroner and told him I thought the thumb might be mine. He thought I was some kind of practical joker and wanted to know if I'd filed a report about it. I told him I had, but only on the Utah side of the lake, where the accident had occurred. The report was never sent to the Wyoming side, so nobody knew about it over there. The coroner checked everything out and called me back about two weeks later. He asked if I could come identify the thumb."

Lindsey obtained the X-rays from his hand surgery and went to the morgue to meet the coroner. The thumb was removed from the cooler, and it perfectly matched Lindsey's hand and the X-rays of his wound.

"The X-rays were important," Lindsey explained, "because I had never been fingerprinted. Everything fit perfectly. Even the cuts from the propeller matched."

The coroner was satisfied and released the thumb to Lindsey, who keeps it in a jar of formaldehyde on a shelf in his closet.

"I was shocked when I heard about an angler finding a human thumb in a fish," Lindsey said. "The acid in a fish's stomach can dissolve a fishhook in a few days, so the angler must have hooked the trout within a few hours after it ate my thumb."

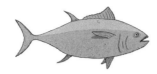

BEACHED BY A TRAFFIC LIGHT

Captain Ed Murray, fisherman extraordinaire of giant tuna, has witnessed many fishing oddities in his years at the helm of fishing boats. Some were firsthand experiences while others were relayed by radio.

"During the tuna season a few years ago," Murray said, "we heard a report of a hookup over the radio. It was from a group of fun-loving fishermen, the nicest bunch you'd ever like to meet. They'd never caught a tuna despite years of fishing. They always seemed to get into some kind of trouble, whether it was getting lost, getting their lines tangled up, or something of the sort."

Murray's wayward fishermen were fishing in dense fog off Montauk, New York, when a fishing reel clattered with the pull of a forceful fish. One of the anglers removed the fishing rod from its holder, set the hook, and began to fight the fish.

"The visibility was less than one hundred feet at the time," Murray said, "so we radioed back to confirm their location."

FISH FACT
Swordfish are born without a sword. As they mature, they lose their teeth and their spiny scales and slowly grow their eponymous nose.

Murray's boat was equipped with a radar system that reported the locations of all incoming radio transmissions. When the tuna-fighting crew reported their location, Murray's radar showed them to be miles from where they reported. Murray was accustomed to the group's ability to get lost, and he quickly radioed back the correction.

"They thought they were fifteen miles southeast of Montauk," Murray said, "but my instruments were showing them to be twelve miles northeast. They were lost, but they told me they didn't care. They had finally hooked their big tuna."

Murray monitored the boat's location and continued to fish. Hours later the fog cleared and the anglers reported their catch.

"After fighting for four hours," Murray said, "the tide changed and these guys discovered that their fish was not a tuna. It was a buoyed lobster pot they had snagged in the fog."

Another unusual occurrence recounted by Murray involved a separate group of fishing acquaintances equally prone to trouble.

The fishermen were returning late one evening from the fishing areas near Montauk. The group was weary and far from home as they approached Freeport, Long Island. They turned toward shore, deciding to dock for the night and resume the trip back the next morning.

"They were nearing their destination," Murray said, "when the chief navigator spotted the first green light marking the passage into port. He soon found the red light that marked the other side of the channel, then another green light, and so on."

The navigator carefully aligned the colored entrance markers and directed the boat toward the center of the channel. The exhausted party of anglers gladly anticipated a calm night's rest inside the harbor, when the boat suddenly lurched, grating to a discomfiting stop. The startled crew looked through the darkness and saw surf casters standing on a beach. The red and green lights were traffic lights along a road that paralleled the shoreline.

You can see how a dark, foggy night would make it easy to mistake a streetlight for a channel marker.

CAT? FISH?

Herchel Saxton and Norman Hollingsworth had been fishing together since they were boys. Mostly they fished for bass in the lakes and creeks that abound in Georgia.

When the two friends grew older, they joined a bass fishing club in the small town of Calhoun. The club organized many annual bass tournaments, and Saxton and Hillingsworth entered them all.

"We were fishing a tournament at Lake Lanier," Saxton said, "and we had gone into one of the small coves to fish for bass along the bank. It was about midnight, and we were using worms."

The two anglers drifted near the shore, eager to hook some of the large bass that hunkered down at night in the shallow water. Hollingsworth carefully soaked his worms in sardine oil before threading them on his hook. It was a technique he had discovered years earlier while snacking on sardines during a slow night of fishing.

"Norm threw out his line, but his worm didn't hit water," Saxton said. "So I said to him, 'You know, you threw your worm up on the bank.' He shook his head and told me he was sure that it had hit the water."

Saxton insisted that Hollingsworth's bait was resting on the bank, but Hollingsworth was adamant. Saxton was trying to explain that there had been no splash when Hollingsworth felt a tug on the line.

"I could see a dark object on the bank taking his worm," Saxton said, "but Norm was sure it was a fish. I told him it was probably a raccoon, but he wouldn't listen."

As Hollingsworth jerked his arm to set the hook, the "fish," instead of swimming toward the boat and into deeper water, traveled away from the boat over the bank. Hollingsworth hollered about a big one and heaved back again on the rod. The "fish" turned and fell from the bank, splashing into the water.

FISH FACT

Moray eels make up for their lack of swallowing strength by secreting a second set of razor-sharp jaws deep in their elongated throats. Once a large prey is grasped using the front teeth, this second set of jaws is launched from the throat to ratchet down the meal.

"When the thing fell in the lake," Saxton said, "Norm knew I was right. He didn't have a fish, but he was awfully excited about hooking whatever it was."

Hollingsworth reeled the unidentified creature halfway to the boat, but it splashed back to the bank and up toward the woods. Repeatedly, he pulled it into the water, and each time it scrambled up the bank.

Ten minutes after the strike, the exhausted creature was within view of Saxton's flashlight.

"Damn if it wasn't a cat," Saxton said. "Its eyes were big and yellow, and it was madder than hell. It must have been wild, and Norm wanted me to pull it in the boat. I told him I'd do no such thing and took my knife and cut the line. I wanted no part of an angry alley cat."

Seconds later, the cat scurried over the bank and disappeared into the woods.

"I've fished for thirty-five years," Saxton said, "and that was the damnedest thing I've ever seen."

Fishermen's bait is like catnip to the strays along the shoreline.

DOUBLE LURE, SINGLE CATCH, GRAND PAYOFF

Trolling a few miles off Cabo San Lucas, Dale Lanyon and Dale Motsinger experienced a once-in-a-lifetime catch. First, Lanyon's bright orange marlin lure was attacked, then seconds later, Motsinger's less colorful mackerel-colored lure was picked up. Both anglers hollered "hookup!" It wasn't long before they realized they were hooked to the same giant fish. For more than 3 hours, the fish stubbornly refused to move 30 to 40 feet from the boat, thrashing its enormous sword.

Eventually, Captain Cessana Chong was able to back the boat close enough for a flying gaff. The marlin was subdued, but not boated. It was too heavy to pull onto the swim step. The captain radioed the Hotel Solmar, and soon a 62-foot yacht with 10 helpers arrived. Still unable to boat the mammoth catch, the captain ordered it lashed to the gunwale. At 9:30 that evening, the boat pulled into the dock and the fish was brought to scale. Except the ropes and scaffolding broke.

A truck was commissioned, but still the fish was so big that its bill hung on the ground. The "official" weight was 957 pounds, but all agreed it was clearly in excess of 1,000 pounds. The pre-

FISH FACT
Thailand is home to some of the largest freshwater fish in the world. Catfish weighing more than a quarter ton, stingrays even larger and heavier. To see incredible photos of these mammoth fish, visit *National Geographic*'s megafish.org.

vious Mexican record was 1,052 pounds, and although this fish was unintentionally landed by two anglers, it most likely would have smashed the record had a correct weight been registered. Regardless, a marlin of this size hitting two separate lures—not live bait—is a rare feat indeed.

RELEASED TODAY, CAUGHT TOMORROW

The first few days of fishing had been productive for Tom and Polly Gillen, owners of *Pizzazz*, a 38-foot Uniflite, captained by Cami Garnier. They were near Cabo San Lucas, Mexico, and had tagged and released three striped marlin and lost a fourth at the strike. Then a north wind began to blow, forcing them back to Cabo San Lucas, where they patiently waited out the five-day storm.

On the sixth day, the weather cleared. Garnier started up the engines and the three headed for the Gorda Banks, a reef 24 miles northeast of Cabo San Lucas. They soon found action and had begun to work a school of dorado when Garnier spotted a striped marlin tailing downswell. Tom took a 12-pound light tackle rig, pinned on live mackerel, and ran to the bow. He flung the bait toward the marlin and waited.

It was a perfect cast. The marlin attacked the bait, and after a 45-minute fight Tom brought the fish alongside the gunwale. Garnier hurried down from the bridge, and when he grabbed the leader, he noticed a tag dangling from the marlin's flank. He removed the old tag, sank a new one, and released the fish unharmed.

FISH FACT
The bones of the needlefish turn bright green when cooked.

Later that afternoon, as they returned to their mooring, Tom inspected the tag. The serial numbers on the shaft looked familiar. He scrounged through their stack of tagging cards and to his wonderment discovered the tag was theirs. It was the same tag they had used six days earlier!

The marlin, showing no signs of the previous battle, had moved from the tip of Baja into the Sea of Cortez 24 miles north. The repeat catch was a spectacular feat and a first in billfishing history.

SALMON, SPEARS, AND BEARS

A full day's boat ride from Juneau, Alaska, sits a secret inlet brimming with spawning salmon. Thousands of sockeye, pink, and a few trout feed off the eggs. Paradise for fishermen, except the shoreline is populated with grizzly bears, and the current gushing down from the alpine lake snowmelt can be deadly. Locals use cast nets to catch fresh fish, obeying the limit for number of fish caught. Nets often snag on rocks and ledges and sink beneath the surface, creating death traps for anyone brave enough or foolish enough to swim in its waters. Two such men, intent on spearing salmon, entered the inlet one warm day in August. Their names have been changed, but their story is true.

"The boat trip to the inlet was uneventful," said Chris Smith. "We saw a few dolphin and some harbor seals. Lots of bald eagles and a couple of whales. But once we anchored and deployed the dinghy, we had our first problem. The outboard wouldn't start. We knew we could paddle upriver to the spot, but the bears would be a problem if we didn't have the power to leave fast. We eventually gave up fixing the motor and decided to take our chances."

Armed with only an air horn for protection from the bears,

Chris and his good friend Larry set up day camp near the water-fall, where the cascading snowmelt swung around the bend of the river like a 10,000-pound blackjack. Chris, a certified dive instructor with years of spearfishing experience, donned his wet suit—a 7.2-millimeter barrier to the 30-degree snow melt. Larry, a local Alaskan, donned a thin 3.2-millimeter summer suit.

"The water was so cold that after each dive, Larry would return to shore and pour hot water into his suit so he could go again."

The pair of spear fishermen had brought a large propane burner and a crab pot to boil gallons of river water throughout the day. Chris entered the water first. The salmon were thick as outback mosquitoes, but only the sockeye were worth shooting. Hundreds of pinks swirled around him. The occasional bright-red sockeye would swim into his vision and then disappear in a crimson flash before he could get a bead on the fish. Powerful eddies pulled against him and the schools of fish. Finally, a sockeye stalled just long enough for a shot. With air fleeing his lungs, Chris pulled the trigger. As he emerged with the first catch of the day, a grizzly appeared on the bank, eyeing the tasty meal.

"Larry saw the bear when I surfaced and used the air horn to scare it away. It worked, and I landed the fish. We caught a few more and continued to scare away the bears when things started to heat up."

FISH FACT
The inches-long mangrove rivulus lives in Florida swampland. This amazing little fish can reproduce without a mate, leap from swamp to swamp, and live out of water for more than 2 months by breathing through its skin.

Unlike with net fishing, these two anglers swam eye-to-eye with their prey. Miles from civilization, and at the mercy of the elements and predators, Chris and Larry spent the next few hours avoiding discarded nets snagged on fallen trees, forceful eddies, and powerful currents that threatened to hurl them downriver like flotsam.

"I've fished in difficult conditions," Chris said, "but nothing like this. Larry, who'd fished here before, easily worked around the dangers, missing snags and spearing fish like an expert, but I was definitely out of my element. Without him, I'd never have had a chance."

By midday the pair had a dozen fish in their cooler and had successfully fought off a steady stream of hungry bears. The tide of good luck, however, was about to change.

"I'd never been that close to a bear," Chris said. "It was early in the afternoon, and I had a nice-sized sockeye, but I was discombobulated with the current when I surfaced near a rocky ledge. A big grizzly was standing there looking at my fish. He was no more than six feet away. We locked eyes. It was as frightening as it was surreal. Larry had told me that the bears only wanted the fish, so

I tried to remember his advice, but with a bear staring at me like that it wasn't easy. He could have easily have jumped in and killed me. But the water was deep, so I knew the bear was waiting for me to come ashore. He didn't want to jump in and swim."

Chris immediately submerged and surfaced around the river bend, his eyes wide with concern. Larry blew the horn. The bear retreated, but then quickly returned. He blew the horn again. The bear disappeared. Satisfied, the two partners switched places and Larry entered the water and quickly landed a fine salmon worth keeping. But the hungry bear had reappeared. This time, when Chris fired the horn, the bear ignored it and headed right toward them.

"Larry knows bears," Chris explained. "He looked at me and then he looked at the bear. He kicked hard to shore and said sternly, 'We gotta go, right now!'"

As the bear closed in, Chris and Larry loaded their gear in record time and feverishly paddled downriver to their boat, an old converted cement-hulled trawler, anchored at the river mouth.

When the fish were cleaned and the beers were opened, both men breathed a thankful sigh of relief, and they headed back to Juneau with a boatload of fish and a story few have ever experienced.

A MARLIN'S LIFE JACKET

Owner of southern California's Balboa Bay Club, Bill Ray, and three of his friends were fishing off Cabo San Lucas, Mexico, when all five fishing reels clacked like a flock of feeding birds. Suddenly the water erupted with five hooked marlin. All four anglers grabbed a fishing rod and silenced the reel's clicker. The air, however, still echoed with chatter. A fifth unattended marlin continued to take line. Ray stepped to the unmanned fishing rod and freed the drag. Then he tied a life jacket to the gear and flung it overboard. An hour later, all four manned marlin were landed and released. Ray, who had kept an eye on the bright orange life jacket, captained the boat as a friend retrieved the floating gear and landed the fifth marlin, releasing it for another day.

FISH FACT
Taiwanese love fishing so much that local entrepreneurs lure customers to high-rise buildings, where large rectangular pools hold schools of hungry shrimp. Customers get to eat what they catch.

A CRIMINAL CATCH

Strange things have happened to Bob Thiry while fishing. One of the most notable incidents involved a mysterious bundle of money.

Thiry had fished Cross Lake for nearly 30 years. Located in Pine City, Minnesota, the 6-mile-long lake brims with fish. Bass, walleye, and Thiry's favorite species, the northern pike, all inhabit the lake.

"I hadn't been on that particular side of the lake for at least four or five years," Thiry said. "And that morning I had this urge to go back over there and fish for northerns and walleyes." Wearing waders, Thiry stood in a few feet of water and cast his lure. When he began to wind the reel, something struck the lure. "I gave the line a jerk, and the way it reacted, I thought I'd hooked a big snapping turtle."

Thiry pulled again, and a shiny brass handle emerged from the water. He reeled the object to the shore, leaned down, and removed a satchel from the hook. It was filled with bundles of uncanceled checks and a stack of "Accounts Receivable" ledger sheets from the local feed mill. Thiry looked at the first check and recognized the name.

"There was no cash, but the checks totaled more than thirteen thousand dollars and the ledger sheets were worth many times more than that to the mill's owner."

Having spent most of his life in the small town of Pine City, Thiry knew everyone there personally—including the owner of the feed mill. "It was very early in the morning when I caught the satchel," he said, "so I went into town and stopped at the bakery for a cup of coffee, and I bumped into the sheriff. I'd been out of town for a few weeks, so I asked him if there had been any recent robberies. He told me there had been two the other night, and one of the robberies was at the Pine City mill. I told him, 'You won't believe this, but I just fished their cotton-pickin' satchel out of the lake!'"

With permission from the sheriff, Thiry took the satchel directly to the mill's owner and asked him if he was having trouble with the law. The puzzled owner stared at him in confusion. Thiry smiled, placed the satchel on the desk, and asked his friend why he would have thrown all of his records into the lake.

"My buddy couldn't believe it," Thiry said. "He was so happy, he nearly went berserk. That was the only ledger he had of all his charge accounts. The find saved him a bundle of money."

The next day, the owner of the mill delivered four quarts of Canadian Club Whisky to Thiry's home. The sheriff was also grateful. The recovered satchel and Thiry's testimony helped convict the robber, who was captured while attempting to cross the Minnesota border into Canada.

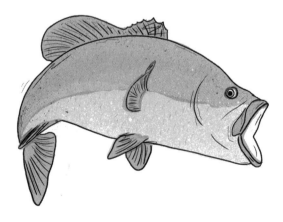

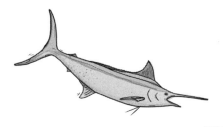

TRIPLE TAG

The charter boat *Run Amock* was fishing the waters off Oyster Reef near Cairns, Australia, when Captain John Phillips's angler Daniel McLeod caught a juvenile black marlin with a tag. The number was S71343. A week later, Captain Phillips caught another small black marlin with a tag. This time it was tag number S71344. Days later, another of Captain Phillips's anglers landed a black marlin. This one, too, was a juvenile, and it, too, had a tag—number S71342. All three consecutively tagged fish had been caught and released by Captain Bill Bilson of the charter boat *Viking*, fishing off Oyster Reef. The three re-tagged and released marlin were part of ninety fish Bilson had tagged that year. The fish may have been small, but no other boat in fishing history has captured three consecutively tagged marlin.

FISH FACT

The largest fish ever caught stand-up style was pulled in by Tracy Melton of Los Alamitos, California. The blue marlin was hooked off Madeira, Portugal, and weighed an astounding 1,083 pounds.

DEAD BODY ON A FLY

Hal Janssen stood waist-deep at the mouth of the San Lorenzo River, where it flows into northern California's Monterey Bay. He was fishing a slow-sinking fly line and a #10 orange-colored fly. The silver salmon had returned to spawn, and they were running thick that December morning.

"I had fished the river the weekend before," Janssen said, "and I knew the salmon were lying in the deep water near the steep bank where the river dumped into the bay. But on that morning, the fish had moved upriver into very shallow water. It was unusual for the fish to be in such shallow water, and they weren't biting."

Unable to hook the shallow-water salmon, Janssen returned to the river mouth, where the fish had been feeding earlier in the week. The other fishermen remained upriver, desperately trying to coax the schooling salmon to strike.

The tide was at its lowest and rising when Janssen waded onto the shallow sandbar and began casting toward the steep bank. After each cast, he allowed the fly line to sink 7 or 8 feet below the surface before beginning his retrieve. At about the sixth cast, he felt something catch the fly.

"All of a sudden, I hooked something," Janssen said. "It didn't really move at first, and when it did, it moved slowly. I thought I'd hooked a large stringer of seaweed brought in from the bay."

Janssen pulled hard in an attempt to break the fishing line, but on each try the heavy object moved only a few feet toward him. "I decided that whatever it was, I'd get it out of the water so no one else would get snagged. The river flowed right by an amusement park at the edge of Monterey Bay, and there was usually some sort of debris around. In fact, earlier that morning another fisherman had hooked a grocery cart."

The incoming tide helped push the heavy weight toward shore, and after 4 or 5 minutes of slowly working the reel, Janssen saw the object emerge 30 feet away.

"I saw something brown that looked like a seal flipper. Commercial fishermen occasionally shot pesky seals, so I thought I'd snagged a dead one."

Janssen patiently retrieved the large object. It descended below the water and surfaced for the second time less than 20 feet away.

"This time I saw a bright pink color," Janssen said. "I kept pulling and the tide kept surging in, and the next moment there was this thing at the tip of my fishing rod. I pulled up hard to get a good look, and I saw what looked like a manikin from a department store. I figured someone had robbed a local store and dumped a manikin into the river."

Suddenly, a swell from the incoming tide lifted the object and dropped it beside Janssen. It was a human body.

"I don't remember getting to the shore," he said. "But there I

was, holding my fly rod and staring in disbelief at the body resting on the sandbar. The fly line was still attached, and I could see my orange fly."

An angler came around the bend and called out to him, but he was too preoccupied to reply. Then a second, familiar voice called out from the levy above the bank of the river.

"A close friend of mine came down to see how the fishing was. He's also a San Jose police officer. I told him what happened, and he ran back to radio for help."

Janssen cut his fishing line and waited for the police to arrive. "I became an immediate suspect," he said. "The first thing the officer in charge wanted me to do was walk back into the river and retrieve the body, which was lying half-submerged on the sandbar. I told him I had dragged the body eighty-five feet across the river and that was as far as I was taking it."

So the policeman ordered another officer into the river. While the officer recovered the body, Janssen answered questions and completed a report.

"I just wanted to leave," Janssen said, "but the police have their procedures. They told me I had to identify the body, which seemed ridiculous to me. I had described the clothing and told them where to find my orange fly, but they wanted me to physically look at the body and identify it as the one I had pulled in. I thought this was crazy. How many bodies did they think were lying in the river with an orange fly hooked to them? I was pretty upset about the whole experience."

Eventually, Janssen returned to the river and identified the body. He also identified his #10 orange fly that was hooked to the gloved hand of the victim.

Soon afterward, he was allowed to leave, but with strict instructions not to move out of state. "I was relieved to get out of there," he said. "I learned later that the victim was a local high school girl who worked at a nearby grocery store and had been missing for a couple of days. Her brown glove was what I thought was a seal's flipper, and the pink color I saw was the jacket she was wearing. A few weeks later a second body was found floating in the bay. It was a male, and in his wallet the police found a photograph of the girl.

"I never found out what had happened, and I was never called to testify at a trial, so I've always assumed the case was never solved."

REELING IN THE DOUGH

The Maryland State Department of Natural Resources planted tracking devices into as many as 3,000 wild largemouth bass in an attempt to follow their migratory and growth patterns. As the years went by, authorities began tracking the fish to a private fish farm. Confused and curious, officials soon discovered that the owner of the farm was buying the illegally captured bass from poachers and then shipping the fish to restaurants around the country and to markets in Asia. By the time the illegal trade was halted, the owner had reportedly made more than $150,000 in profit. He was charged with trafficking in the interstate sale of a protected species and faced more than 5 years in prison and a $250,000 fine.

Three South Auckland fishermen were charged with smuggling a frozen 30-pound red snapper into a local cash tournament. Local officials tested the fish and the supposed bait used to catch it. But the bait turned out to be fresher than the catch, leading to the contestants' arrest. In fact, the winning fish was determined to be at least 2 weeks old and was probably caught by the three men and frozen prior to the tournament. All three forfeited the $9,600 prize money and faced jail time and fines.

Loading bass from a cage into a boat's live well isn't as unusual as you might think. A fisherman in Indiana was caught by a police video camera doing just that in the Tippecanoe Valley Anglers Tournament. And back in 1983, a Louisiana angler's $105,000 win in a Bass Anglers Sportman Society (B.A.S.S.) tournament was later disqualified even after he passed a polygraph test. Footage from hidden cameras caught him wet-handed as he transferred the winning fish from a trap into his boat. But one of the worst tournament cheats was at a Virginia event, where an angler was observed climbing aboard his boat in a raincoat cinched tightly around his neck. Beneath the slicker were two stringers of winning bass previously caught, which the participant planned to dump into the live well when his fishing partner was distracted.

When Great Britain competitor Matthew Clark stood in front of the cameras and accepted his first-place check for 800 pounds, the crowd cheered. His bass was a lunker at 13 pounds and easily outweighed the competition in the annual Bailiwick Bass Club Open. That is, until local bass fisherman Shane Bentley

FISH FACT

Reef fish larvae can float as far as 100 miles from home. Some, like baby cardinal fish, find their way back by sense of smell. Apparently, reefs give off a strong underwater odor.

spotted something familiar. Bentley had recently visited the nearby St. Peter Port Aquarium, where he'd seen a similarly sized fish swimming in one of the tanks. Both fish had unusual markings across their foreheads. Bentley returned to the aquarium and alerted the director, who soon discovered the bass was missing. Local police were called, and Clark was arrested. Turns out, the tournament cheater was desperate to pay off a large debt, so he broke into the aquarium at night by scaling an adjacent cliff with a rope ladder. After a thorough investigation, Clark admitted to the theft and was fined 100 hours of community service. He was also forbidden to enter future local fishing tournaments.

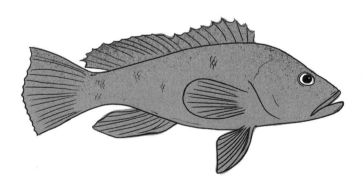

RATTLESNAKE RAINBOW

"**M**y husband and I were forest rangers in Michigan," 80-year-old Mrs. Spears explained, "and we had this secret spot on our favorite stream where I liked to fish, especially for trout.

"One day I decided to try a new place on the other side of the stream. So I crossed the nearest bridge and walked until I found a break in the brush. I made it to the riverbank, and on my first cast, got a nice strike. It was a little twelve-inch keeper, and as I lifted it from the water, I heard a loud buzzing behind me. I knew right away it was a rattlesnake. I froze, with the trout hugged tightly to my chest. The snake kept rattling its tail, and the fish slipped through my fingers and dropped inside the front of my blouse. I knew if I moved, the snake would strike. So I gritted my teeth and stood there, as the fish flopped around inside my blouse.

"Finally, after a minute or so, I didn't hear the rattling, and I glanced over my shoulder and saw

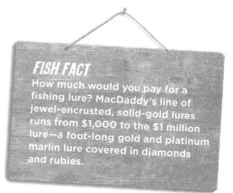

FISH FACT
How much would you pay for a fishing lure? MacDaddy's line of jewel-encrusted, solid-gold lures runs from $1,000 to the $1 million lure—a foot-long gold and platinum marlin lure covered in diamonds and rubies.

that the snake was crawling up the path away from me. I immediately started feeling inside my blouse for the fish. Just then, a fisherman broke through the brush and froze at the sight of me. I don't know if he saw the rattlesnake in the path or just me fighting to get that fish out of my blouse, but the man dropped all his gear and ran back into the brush.

"I eventually freed the fish, and once the snake was safely off the path, called out for the man to return for his stuff. He came back and we had a good laugh.

"To this day, that was the scariest and funniest moment I've ever had in a lifetime of fishing."

RAINING FISH

FISHING FOR THE TRUTH

When rain came to the tee boxes of the Salisbury Golf Club in Wiltshire, England, it dumped more than rain. Bouncing off the closely cropped grass were koi and goldfish. Carl Horrax, manager of the old course, at first thought it was a gag, until he saw the amount of fish pouring down from the sky. Course member Michael Cartwright was also flummoxed. But later that day, scientists confirmed that a waterspout had sucked the fish from a nearby pond and transferred the swirling critters to the golf course. They also explained that these watery mini tornadoes had transported frogs and even crabs to lawns and parks.

FISH FACT
A short list of surprises found in the bellies of just-caught fish: a live rattlesnake was found in the belly of a largemouth bass; a huge cobia contained an empty can of beer; a halibut held two sea horses; a black sea bass had a turtle; and a striped bass had an entire lobster.

TWO TROPHY BASS ON ONE LINE

It was a Father's Day that Mike Bledsoe will never forget. He and his 8-year-old son, Jacob, left home that June morning in 1993 for a day of bass fishing at Lake Casitas in Ojai, California. Just before daybreak, they slid their 16-foot aluminum bass boat into the water and drove across the lake to one of their favorite fishing spots.

They had been fishing for about an hour, when Bledsoe cast his plug across a shallow point in the lake and began a slow retrieve.

"I had just started reeling when I got a hit," Bledsoe said. "It was a big fish, and it came clear out of the water. I went to set the hook and I missed him."

The plug fell from the fish's mouth and skidded across the water. Bledsoe was quickly reeling in the excess line when the fish suddenly struck again.

"There was a huge splash," Bledsoe said, "and we could see the size of the bass. I thought I had him, because I felt the weight, but a few seconds after I set the hook, the fish hit again. I turned to Jake and said, 'What am I doing wrong?' I had never experienced anything like that before."

Bledsoe set the hook for the third time, still uncertain whether he could hook the oddly behaving bass.

"That's when I really felt the weight," Bledsoe said. "The fish took off and never broke water again."

Bledsoe told Jacob to reel in his line and get ready to net a large bass.

FISH FACT
Fish cannot move their tongues.

"The bass fought hard," Bledsoe said, "but it wasn't the tremendous fight I thought it would be. There was more deadweight than anything."

Bledsoe hoped the bass weighed more than 10 pounds. He had caught many 8- and 9-pound bass before, but a 10-pounder was a trophy fish. He also wanted to fulfill his promise to Jacob, the promise to mount any bass that weighed 10 pounds or more.

Not until the catch was near the boat did Bledsoe see that two bass were hooked to the plug—one to the front treble hook, the other to the back hook. They were swimming in tandem, and both were large fish.

"When I saw how big they were, I backed off on the drag and let them run again. I didn't want to lose them."

After a short run, Bledsoe tightened the drag and eased the two bass to the boat. Jacob waited patiently, and then, with one swift scoop, netted both fish.

"Jake did a great job getting the fish into the net," Bledsoe said. "He wasn't strong enough to get both of them into the boat, so I laid down my rod and we lifted them together. We were so excited, our knees were shaking."

They put the fish in the live well and returned to the lakeside for an official weight. One bass weighed 12 pounds even. The other weighed 11 pounds, 12 ounces. Both were trophy fish caught with one cast.

"We couldn't believe it," Bledsoe said. "All the way back to the dock, we kept opening the live well and looking at those two fish. Jake and I really wanted a ten-pound bass, but we never dreamed of catching two at the same time."

A ROOSTERFISH TO CROW ABOUT

Roosterfish have an unusual dorsal fin. The jagged skin spikes upward like the comb of a rooster. Baja California is home to the world record—a 114-pounder caught back in 1960. Few anglers since then have caught anything close. In fact, only a handful have ever landed a 90-pounder. Ten-year-old Keith de Fiebre is one of those few.

Early one Baja California morning, de Fiebre, along with his mom and brother and a good friend, chartered a boat captained by Manuel Ortiz. He was their favorite local captain, and he always managed to find fish for them. The plan was to target roosterfish in the morning and then head toward deeper water for marlin. Captain Ortiz drove directly to the stretch of open beach off the Punta Arenas lighthouse, and soon roosterfish were spotted crashing the surface after bait. But after 2 hours of slow-trolling live bait, not a single fish had been hooked. De Fiebre asked Captain Ortiz to stop the boat and drift. A fresh live mullet was rigged and tossed overboard. Minutes later, the mullet peeled line from the reel.

"Hey, I've got one!" de Fiebre yelled, letting the fish take the line without setting the hook. He'd caught many roosters before and knew they were notorious for mouthing the bait without swallowing it.

"Now!" Captain Ortiz yelled as de Fiebre reared back against the fishing rod. The drag complained loudly as the hooked fish headed to open ocean. The boat had drifted 600 yards offshore, and Captain Ortiz turned and followed the fish. Suddenly, the roosterfish spun 180 degrees and raced toward the shore, slowing in the breaking waves. Captain Ortiz spun the boat and backed dangerously close to the sand, waves sloshing over the transom.

The roosterfish raced along the shoreline, and de Fiebre, exhausted by the power of the fish, hollered for help. His best friend reached around de Fiebre's shoulders and helped him keep pressure on the fish. For 45 minutes, the fish fought relentlessly. Finally, it tired and came close enough to the boat for the deckhand to secure it with a gaff, yelling excitedly in Spanish.

"Muy grande!" Captain Ortiz barked happily as he helped boat the huge rooster.

Too large for the fish box, the roosterfish hung out both ends. Later, back at the beach, the fish was weighed on an old, rusty scale and it measured 95 pounds even. It was caught on 20-pound-test monofilament line and was unofficially the fourth-largest roosterfish ever caught by an angler.

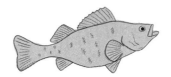

DOG FISH

FISHING FOR
THE TRUTH

Leon Hale of the *Houston Chronicle* blogged an ice-fishing story that took place on Lake St. Clair, Michigan. Anglers were fishing for yellow perch from their shanties when a man ran out on the ice, hollering for help. Apparently, his dog had plunged into their ice hole in pursuit of a big northern pike. The Irish setter was quickly whisked beneath the surface of the ice, sure to drown. That is, until moments later, when a nearby angler came running out

> **FISH FACT**
> Large electric rays can produce up to 200 volts of electricity. But much like a battery, the ray's ability to generate this powerful shock diminishes after repeated use, forcing it to rest as it recharges.

of his shanty, chased by a soaking-wet Irish setter. The dog had managed to find a second ice hole and climb free.

Irene Sommer was walking her two dachshund puppies along the banks of a small lake near the town of Mönchengladbach, Germany, when an enormous splash drenched the dogs and

Sommer. A gigantic catfish had spied the furry bait and attacked. Sommer raced toward the water, screaming, as the catfish tried to backswim into the lake with one of the dachshunds firmly clenched in its jaws. Juergen Schmidt, local park ranger, heard the commotion and turned to see the splashing fish attempting to pull the terrified puppy into the lake. By the time he arrived, Sommer had extricated her dog from the maws of the giant predator. Both witnesses estimated the catfish to be 4 feet long with a massive whiskered jaw.

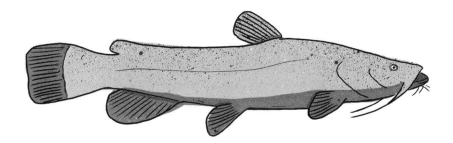

IMPOSSIBLE CAPE COD TARPON

The sun was setting on a warm August afternoon on Cape Cod, Massachusetts, when 16-year-old Michael Mealey threaded a dead red snapper to his fishhook. He and his younger sister, Alice, were surf fishing Allen Harbor Beach near the rock jetty that marked the entrance to the boat harbor. They hoped the dead snapper would attract a small sand shark or stingray. As the sky filled with purplish orange light, Michael noticed a light tap on the end of the 7-foot surf rod.

"When the rod moved," he said, "I took it out of the sand spike and waited to set the hook. It wasn't a very big strike, so I thought it was a small sand shark. I was waiting for another nibble when I felt a big hit. I yanked back, and about ten seconds later, the fish jumped. It was big, but because it was getting dark, I couldn't see what kind of fish it was."

The fish splashed back to the water and charged the boat harbor and the jagged rocks of the jetty. It was low tide, so Michael ran along the slippery rocks. He was barefoot, but managed not to slip as the fish rounded a warning buoy marking the shallow entranceway.

"My line was bent around the post of the marker buoy and I

thought for sure it would just snap. Luckily, I got around the buoy. The fish jumped, and then, after about twenty minutes, it headed across the channel into deeper water. There were boats coming home and Alice and I were yelling for them not to cross the line."

Incoming boats stopped to watch the young angler fight his fish. Other boats navigated around the fishing line.

"I was putting as much pressure as I could on the fifteen-pound-test line," Michael continued. "But my reel only had a hundred and fifty yards on it and the fish had nearly spooled me a few times. After that first twenty minutes, I had it close to shore, but when it hit the surf, it turned and bolted back to deeper water, taking all the line in a fast run. I thought for sure I would lose him."

FISH FACT

Piranhas are excellent game fish. Powerful fighters, piranhas actively attack lures. They are also excellent table fare, with firm white flesh.

By then, dozens of boat captains had stopped to watch, and sixty or more people had congregated on the shore. The seaweed-covered rocks were slippery and sharp, and Michael's feet and knees were bleeding from multiple falls.

"This nice woman was on vacation from Germany and she followed me around, bandaging up all my cuts with pieces of a torn T-shirt," Michael said. "My feet were really bad. They were so cut up that after the fight I could barely walk for days."

The battle continued for more than an hour before the mystery fish finally slowed. Michael cranked the reel and watched the large shadow slide into the shallows. Alice, who had borrowed a gaff from a house nearby, handed it to her brother.

"I was waist-deep, and it took me four or five tries before I got the gaff through the fish's thick scales. Then I pulled hard and dragged it from the rocks up to the beach about a hundred yards away. It was huge and unlike any fish I had ever hooked. I didn't know it at the time, but the people who loaned us the gaff had called our parents. As I got to the sand, my mom and dad drove up."

To everyone's amazement, the mystery fish was a tarpon, something that had never been caught on Cape Cod.

"I iced the fish overnight, and the following morning we had it weighed and measured. It was five feet long and weighed in at fifty-two pounds even. It was crazy to catch a huge tarpon like that from the shore. But even better was the fact that it was also the first tarpon ever caught by rod and reel on the Cape. Even though I did it, I still can't believe it really happened."

JAYWALKING CARP

Officer Alvin Yamaguchi of the California Highway Patrol parked his car in the middle of a flooded intersection in Irvine's city center. It had been raining for days in southern California, and many of the major thoroughfares were closed to traffic. Smaller roads carried the overflow, but these, too, were beginning to fill with water.

"It was late in the afternoon," Officer Yamaguchi said, "and the rain wasn't letting up. One of our freeways was under four feet of water and commuters were using Irvine Boulevard, which parallels the freeway. Rattlesnake Canyon Reservoir, a few miles up in the hills, had overflowed onto the boulevard. I was dispatched in case the road flooded and the traffic needed rerouting."

When Yamaguchi arrived, Irvine Boulevard was a foot and a half under water. Vehicles were stalled and traffic was clogged for miles. Large chunks of debris floated down the middle of the 100-foot-wide road. Yamaguchi and his partner donned their rain suits and stepped into the submerged intersection to divert the tangled traffic.

"I had been standing in the intersection for only a few minutes," Yamaguchi said, "when my partner started hollering at me to come over to the other side of the patrol car. I thought something was wrong, and I ran around the car to see what was happening. My partner was pointing at a fish, yelling, 'It's a bass! It's a bass!'"

Yamaguchi looked to where his partner was pointing. A large fish was splashing its way down the middle of the road. Yamaguchi waited until the fish floated by, then reached down with both hands and scooped it into his arms.

"It was a thirty-pound carp," Yamaguchi said, "and I didn't know what to do with it. I had it in a bear hug, and I was standing knee-deep in the middle of the intersection. All I could think to do was handcuff it to the bumper of the patrol car."

He located a pair of plastic Flex-Cuffs and secured one end through the carp's mouth. He cinched the other end to the car's bumper. Motorists driving by waved and laughed at the unusual sight. Others called their local police departments.

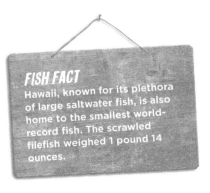

FISH FACT
Hawaii, known for its plethora of large saltwater fish, is also home to the smallest world-record fish. The scrawled filefish weighed 1 pound 14 ounces.

"The word traveled fast," Yamaguchi said. "My fellow officers started calling on the radio to confirm the rumor. Nobody could believe it. The carp had come all the way down from the Rattlesnake Canyon Reservoir. Luckily, one of the city employees who was working at the intersection had a Polaroid camera and took a picture of me holding the fish."

The next day Yamaguchi gave the photograph to the Police Department's Public Affairs Office for an article that had been written for the local newspaper. The story was sent by wire to papers across the country, and within days he was a celebrity.

"If I'd known all this was going to happen," he said, "I would never have given the carp away. I would have taken it home and stuffed it."

Five months later, Yamaguchi was contacted by the Bill Cosby company, and within weeks he was flown to Philadelphia to appear on Cosby's game show *You Bet Your Life*. During the show, he recounted his unusual fishing story and, in the process, won $13,500 in prize money. It was one of the largest wins in the show's history.

"I'm still surprised by all the interest it caused," Yamaguchi said. "I used to think of carp as garbage fish, but not anymore."

MILLION-DOLLAR GAFF

The appeal of fishing is not just the size and type of fish caught, but the mystery of what's been hooked. I've personally come across two bales of marijuana while fishing the Sea of Cortez. Both finds were quickly returned to the water.

Raymond Lucas's discovery, however, was boated. It was during a day of flounder fishing when Lucas spotted a blue satchel floating in the waters off Jamaica Bay, New York. He grabbed a gaff and boated the flotsam. When he peered inside, he saw a fortune. He raced back to the dock and called his good friend, Frank LaSpisa, who confirmed the catch of $5,000,000 in negotiable bonds. Rather than attempt some nefarious sale of the lucrative catch, Lucas contacted the New York Police Department, whose detectives eventually traced the money to a local delivery firm. Officials at the firm were flummoxed. No report of the lost bonds had been provided from the Korean company that issued the bonds. Lucas was given a receipt for the money and told to wait three years. If no one claimed the bonds, the money was his.

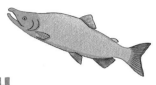

 BEAR CATCH

For more than 30 years, Dr. John Craighead has studied bears. He is the world's leading expert on grizzly bear behavior, and is credited with pioneering the practice of capturing, color-marking, and radio-tracking bears. Craighead is also an avid fisherman, so it was no surprise that this world-renowned bear expert caught a bear on rod and reel.

It was summertime in Alaska, 1980, and Craighead and his daughter, Karen, stood near a waterfall on the shore of the Brooks River in Katmai National Park and Preserve. They were there to observe Alaska brown and grizzly bears gathering at the falls to feed on migrating salmon. On this morning, no bears were present, so the Craigheads spent the free time fishing for their daily dinner of sockeye salmon.

"We were fishing a spot where the brown bears aggregate to catch salmon," Craighead said. "The salmon move up the Brooks River and are temporarily stopped by a falls. This makes the salmon more readily available to the bears and provides many opportunities for us to observe them."

Craighead quickly caught two salmon and was playing a third when, on the opposite side of the river 100 yards downcurrent, he saw a brown bear emerge from the timber. The bear entered the water and forded the river.

"Over the years," Craighead said, "the local bear population learned that the sound of a splashing fish or a screeching reel meant an easy meal. The bears would approach a fisherman, usually a tourist from another country, who would then drop his pole and retreat into the alders, leaving the fish he had caught lying on the bank."

As Craighead played his salmon, the bear exited the river and ambled toward him and his daughter. Concerned that the bear would smell the two fish lying at his feet, Craighead told Karen to wrap the fish in a plastic bag and place them inside his backpack.

"At the spot where I was fishing," Craighead said, "the water was about twenty feet deep. Behind me the vegetation of spruce and alder was impenetrable, so the only way out was along the bank toward the bear. I told Karen to stand behind me and get her camera ready because I thought she might get some interesting pictures."

FISH FACT

All fish have scales, but some fish, like the tunas, have such small scales as to be almost invisible.

Craighead's salmon had jumped a few times but remained well downstream. The bear continued along the bank, then suddenly plunged into the river 75 feet from where the Craigheads stood. It swam after the hooked salmon, pawed it, and turned back toward shore. Craighead's rod bowed forward and the line pulled from the reel.

"I had the bear on the line for thirty seconds or more," Craighead said, "but of course there was nothing I could do. When the bear reached the bank, I tightened the drag and broke the line."

The bear entered the heavy brush and began to eat the freshly caught salmon. The Craigheads quickly assembled their gear and started along the bank. Their only escape was downriver past the feeding bear.

"I wanted to get out of there before the bear finished the salmon and came after our other two fish," Craighead said. "I knew we didn't have much time. As we passed the spot where the bear had disappeared, we could hear him feeding on our salmon." They held on to their two salmon and made record time back to camp, leaving the bear behind.

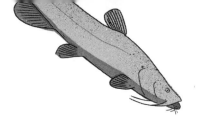

CATFISH BLUE JEANS

Duard Boone from Kansas City, Missouri, fished every summer with his grandfather Arthur Tucker Boone, a local farmer and dedicated fisherman. During one of their many catfish excursions, Arthur told Duard the following story, which Duard related.

"Every morning for several years, my grandfather walked by his favorite fishing hole in a creek that ran through his farm. One day, he noticed two very large catfish lingering around a cave in the banks of the creek. He was wearing only long johns and overalls, but he decided to ride his horse out and wade into the water to capture those two big catfish.

"He stopped the horse near a grove of trees and cut two timber branches at just the right length. He took off his overalls, and in just his long johns, he slipped into the water just above the fish, and moved slowly, forcing them back inside the cave. He submerged the tree branches and poked inside the cave until the fish attacked. One after another, the fish latched on to the branches and Arthur was able to grab them by the gills. That's when he realized he had no way of transporting them from the creek back to the house.

"He carefully hauled them to the bank, and, while pinning them to the mud with his body, was able to grab his discarded overalls and tie the bottom of each leg closed. Then he slid a catfish into each leg. He secured the fish, then dragged the heavy overalls to his horse, slung them over the horse's back, and rode home.

"He was the greatest fisherman I've ever known. He taught me how to fish, and he taught me about life and responsibility. And he always had a tale to tell. I loved him dearly."

SWALLOWED!

It sounds like a great advertisement. John Bembers was fishing from a boat on Lake Michigan when he dropped his watch overboard. Three years later, Thomas Kresnak discovered the watch, which was still ticking, inside the belly of a 42-pound salmon.

Here's a story for the class reunion: Joe Richardson lost his class ring during a Texas fishing trip to Lake Sam Rayburn. Twenty-one years later, it was recovered in the belly of an 8-pound bass.

Label your belongings! In Stockholm, Sweden, a fisherman harvesting wild mussels in the cold Norwegian Sea was shucking his catch, when he came across an engagement ring engraved with its owner's name. The ring was returned to its grateful owner, Bengt Wingstedt, who had lost it overboard two years earlier.

Nearsighted monkfish: While leaning over the rail of a boat off the Belgian coast, Gosselin Deleus lost his prescription glasses. A month later, the glasses were discovered in the belly of a monkfish. Deleus learned of the discovery while reading a local fishing magazine that had reported the catch. Deleus contacted the fisherman, who returned the glasses.

A two-ring tale: Leon Hale of the *Houston Chronicle* reported that a man fishing outside of Freeport, Texas, in the Gulf of Mexico lost an heirloom ring overboard while fishing for snapper.

The ring had been passed down from generation to generation and contained his great-grandfather's initials, JHC, on the inside of the band. A year later, that same fisherman was cleaning a catch of snapper, when he spotted a ring inside one of the fish bellies. Unfortunately, it was not his ring. But it was engraved with initials and the name of a small high school in Illinois. The fisherman contacted the school and was able to track the ring's owner, a very nice young woman. The two began corresponding and eventually married. Years later, they were visiting San Francisco and stopped at a fishmonger's shop in Chinatown. On a shelf near the back of the shop was a collection of objects for sale—objects the fishmonger had found inside the bellies of the fish he

FISH FACT
An oyster can lay as many as 500 million eggs a year.

sold. There were money clips, military dog tags, miscellaneous jewelry, pocketknives, coins, and yes, an heirloom ring with the initials JHC engraved on the inner band.

Chomping cod: A Dutchman by the name of Cor Stoop was on a North Sea fishing trip aboard the *Hendrik Karssen* when he felt a little queasy. Soon the queasiness turned to seasickness. One thing led to another, and suddenly Stoop was missing his false teeth. Three months later, an angler fishing aboard the same charter boat in nearby waters caught a 19-pound cod. While cleaning the fish, the angler noticed something odd protruding from the cod's stomach. The skipper of the *Hendrik Karssen* was alerted and—you guessed it—he remembered the trip three months earlier when Stoop had lost his teeth. The incredible catch was reported on local radio and Stoop's dentures were soon returned.

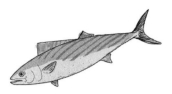

KNIFING FOR BONITO

James Blevins and his brother, John, were excited to fish the King Harbor jetty off Redondo Beach, California. The bonito were rumored to be running, and the brothers had prerigged their fishing rods with their favorite iron jigs.

"When we got to the rocks," James explained, "we could see several anglers already hooked into the bonito. They had heavier gear, and we knew with our lighter line, it wouldn't be long before we were landing fish."

Thirty minutes later, as the other anglers pulled bonito after bonito from the water, the brothers had yet to get a strike.

"I told John we should change colors," James said. "But still no bonito. By now more anglers were hooking up on each side of us and we hadn't even had a bump from a fish. We were beginning to feel rejected."

James set his fishing rod on the rocks and wandered among the successful anglers. What he saw were bright chrome lures. Lots and lots of shimmering silver jigs without extra color or feathers.

FISH FACT
The heart of a blue whale is approximately the size of a Volkswagen Beetle.

Worried, he hurried back to his brother to report the bad news.

"We had chrome lures, but every one of them had extra colors and no bonito would touch them."

Dejected, the brothers slumped to the jetty and watched as the other fishermen continued to land fish.

"That's when John pulled out a little chrome penknife with two small blades and a hole at each end for a key ring. He gave me a sheepish look and said it was the only thing he had that was solid chrome."

Desperate and out of options, John hunkered down in the rocks so the other anglers couldn't watch his last-ditch effort. He quickly removed the hooks from one of his lures, and then slipped the hooks through the holes in the knife and handed the makeshift lure to James.

"I felt kind of bad giving it to my brother," John said, "but I was embarrassed and didn't think it would work. I guess I just didn't want the other guys to see me cast a little pocketknife into the fish. I should have been more confident, because it worked!"

On the first cast, his brother hooked a fish. Then another, and another. By the time he made his third cast, James was digging into his pocket for his pocketknife key ring. Within minutes, John, too, was hooked to a bonito.

"We hooked more bonito than anyone else on the jetty that day," he said. "We also found that by opening

the blades up a little bit, we could get more action from the knives. Soon, the other anglers were asking what we were using and we showed them our knives. All of them started digging into their tackle boxes and pockets for similar key rings."

After one of the best days of fishing, the brothers stopped at the local tackle shop for some buck knives. After all, albacore season was just around the corner.

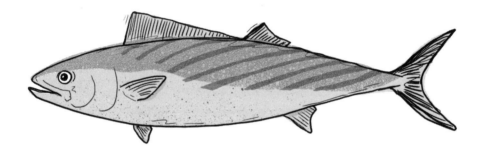

FISHING FOR THE TRUTH

LASSOED TUNA

When Ernie Carreiro left his shop on Commercial Street in Provincetown, Massachusetts, little did he know he would land a huge bluefin tuna.

Carreiro was walking with his wife when he spotted a flurry of water near shore. At first he thought it was a school of bluefish—until he saw the wide back of a tuna. The fish was circling in the shallow water, seemingly disoriented. Carreiro looked around and saw a beached lobster trap with a stretch of rope. He grabbed the rope and tied a loose lasso. He threw out the line, and on the third attempt, the loop landed over the fish's tail. Carreiro hauled back and the fish pulled him out to a shallow sandbar. Two nearby anglers, Joe Andrews and Jimmy Santos, joined in the fight from their skiff. The three men soon pulled the fish aboard, and then hurried to the P-Town dock to sell the valuable fish.

FROZEN TO THE LAKE

It was a typically cold winter's day in central Maine when fishing guide Greg Trefethen and a pal were drilling holes with a power auger through the thick ice on Long Pond. Rumors of fat lake trout had both men willing to brave the freezing temperature, but as the mercury dropped, they were eager to bait their hooks, set their traps, and return to the relative comfort of their nearby ice shanty.

Trefethen, who wore prosthetic legs after losing both while stationed aboard a naval vessel that ran afoul of a particularly powerful typhoon, quickly bored their first hole, but as he began to remove the heavy auger, a fountain of icy water surged from the hole and sloshed over his prosthetic feet. As Trefethen worked the auger free of the ice and set it on the snow, he realized something was wrong. His feet had frozen in place. Literally.

Unable to move, Trefethen called out to his friend to hurry to the shanty and retrieve a hammer

FISH FACT
During mating season, schools of singing toadfish release a hum so loud that boaters in Sausalito, California, complained to authorities. The sound was compared to the drone of an aircraft.

and chisel. Minutes later, the men began to hammer and chip away at Trefethen's artificial toes. Halfway through the ordeal, a local ranger checking for fishing licenses spied the unusual scene and hurried to help.

"As the ranger closed in," Trefethen said, "I decided it would be funny to play a practical joke on him. These guys are usually pretty bored this time of year, so I started screaming in pain. I yelled out that I was losing my feet to frostbite. His eyes widened and he rushed up to us. That's when I unhinged my legs and dropped to the ice. He was so shocked he didn't think to ask for our fishing licenses, which was a good thing because my buddy's license was expired and he hadn't renewed it yet."

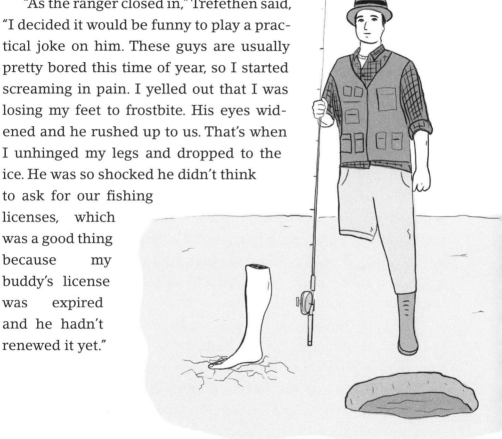

DORADO RECAPTURED

Richard Lenyk and his good friend Rob Olson traveled south from their homes in southern California to Baja California's famed Las Arenas Hotel for a few days of *panga* fishing. It was December and the weather was cool.

"It was a windy day," Lenyk said, "so we stayed close to shore. We got into a small school of dorado that were putting on a fantastic aerial display. Rob and I were hooking fish on every cast."

Earlier in the day, Olson had rigged up a light rod spooled with 8-pound-test line, a 30-pound leader, and a shiny gold swivel in hopes of some light-gear fishing. But the dorado were so thick, he never switched gear, and instead offered the lighter outfit to the guide. The guide quickly baited the hook and cast the offering to the hungry school.

"The guide quickly hooked up," Lenyk said, "and just as quickly broke off on the light line. He switched to heavier gear and was soon catching dorado with us. We stayed with the school for about an hour, drifting with the current until the bite shut off. The guide started up the engine, and moved off to another spot thirty or forty minutes upwind, miles from dorado action."

The group baited their hooks and started fishing, and were soon in another hungry school of dorado.

"I hooked up to a good-sized dorado" Lenyk said, "and fought it for a short time. When it was to the boat, the guide reached over and gaffed it and pulled it into the *panga*. None of us could believe our eyes."

The dorado was a keeper, and in its mouth was a length of 30-pound leader, light 8-pound-test fishing line, and a shiny gold swivel.

"I used to always buy the black swivels," Lenyk said, "but after that day gold became my color of choice."

A CHAMPION IS A CHAMPION

A seven-year-old named Champion Rankin holds the 29-pound, 12-ounce king salmon he caught on Pere Marquette Lake in Michigan.

AWESOME VICTORIES, RECORD-SETTING CATCHES

THE STING OF VICTORY

Caught in Otehei Bay, New Zealand, this 425-pound stingray measured 8½ feet from head to tail and 6½ feet from wingtip to wingtip. This onetime world record was landed by Bill Bendall (left) while at anchor aboard Capt. Snooks Fuller's charter boat *Lady Doreen*.

TWINS' ALL-TACKLE WORLD RECORDS

Twin brothers Adam and Sean Konrad have been pulling massive fish from Saskatchewan's Lake Deifenbaker for more than a decade. First a 15-pound rainbow trout, then a 20-pounder, and soon the new Saskatchewan provincial record. But they were just getting started.

The brothers, who work day jobs as automotive technicians in Saskatoon, were soon learning the area, working lures across promising spots, and devising strategies for big fish.

"Once we started getting twenty-pound fish, we knew we were onto something," Adam said. "And so we targeted the provincial record, which at the time stood at twenty-seven and a half pounds."

On June 17, 2006, while fishing a favorite location on the lake, both brothers hooked up simulta-neously at opposite ends of their boat. Sean landed a 20-pound rainbow, which he quickly released, while Adam fought a lunker from the bow. After a long bat-tle with the fish, the brothers boated a 28½-pound rainbow and set the new Saskatchewan record.

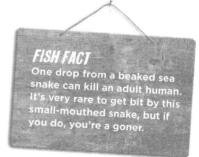

FISH FACT
One drop from a beaked sea snake can kill an adult human. It's very rare to get bit by this small-mouthed snake, but if you do, you're a goner.

"After we got the local record, we decided to try for the world record," Sean explained. "I caught a thirty-pound trout the following weekend, and I knew then that we had a chance at breaking the 1970 forty-two-pound record."

The next weekend, the brothers, along with two good friends, Ben and Shane, headed out in pursuit of a monster rainbow. Three hours into the trip, Adam hooked a mammoth fish.

"As it came out of the water for its first jump, all of our mouths dropped open at its size," Adam said.

The fish took 50 yards of line in a single run, and when it finally tired, Adam realized their net was too small. With the fish alongside the boat, Ben and Shane held Sean's legs as he plunged beneath the surface and pulled the fish into the boat by hand. The fish weighed 33.3 pounds, a world record on 12-pound-test line, but still not the all-tackle record they were hoping for.

Adam and Sean, inspired by the size of their latest fish, continued fishing throughout the summer, releasing everything smaller than a world record.

"We ran into some amazing fish," Adam said. "A thirty-one-pound lake trout, a sixteen-and-a-half-pound burbot, countless ten-pound walleye, and many twenty-plus-pound northern pike.

We even landed another world record, a thirty-four-and-a-half-pound rainbow trout that broke the former eight-pound line class record."

But the all-tackle world record eluded them. Until June 5, 2007, when the brothers were fishing a favorite stretch of shoreline around 9:30 in the evening.

"I launched my Mepps Syclops lure and was slowing my retrieval, focusing on the lure presentation, when I felt a thump on the line. I set the hook, but the fish wouldn't move. I was using six-pound test, so I loosened the drag and waited. That's when I felt the tail start to wag. Then he started to roll. My arms were burning by now, and I was keeping my line as high as possible. I yelled to Sean that I thought I had a thirty-pounder."

The fight lasted 12 minutes before they saw the fish, then another 10 minutes before the fish began to slow.

"I knew it was the largest rainbow I had ever seen," Adam said. "I loosened the drag again, hoping the lighter tension would avoid its tail snapping the line, which happened all the time on light line."

Adam waded into the water waist-deep and cradled the fish in his hands before grasping it by the lip and trying to hoist it into the air. But the fish was too heavy, and Adam's arms were too tired from the fight.

"I could feel the weight of it. My arms went numb and my mind was clouded with exhaustion, but before my arms fell and the fish swam away, I knew that my goal had been reached."

Two years later, on September 9, 2009, history was made once

Adam and Sean Konrad and their 48-pound rainbow trout.

again, when Sean hooked a monster trout on his Jointed Rapala. It was 11:00 p.m. and the brothers were riding a wave of newfound fame. They'd set numerous line class records and were busy guiding an elite roster of clients for once-in-a-lifetime rainbows. But on this night, it was just the two brothers out looking for lunkers.

"Sean hooked something big," Adam recalled, "but it never jumped. It would take these long runs, maybe thirty or forty yards, again and again. Then after about twenty minutes, it came to the boat and rolled onto its side. We knew it was spent, so we boated it and knew it was a record."

Not only was it a record, but the new all-tackle world record for rainbow trout, weighing in at 48 pounds even. Since then Sean has also broken the all-tackle burbot world record. And while the trout fishing has dwindled on Lake Deifenbaker, the twins continue to guide in their spare time.

"The fishing has slowed, but big ones are still out there," Adam said.

For more information and photos, visit fishinggeeks.com.

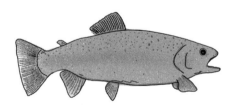

BEACHING A BILLFISH BAREHANDED

Hayden McDowell vaulted from the sand and ran toward the shore. A mysterious fin had appeared 30 feet from shore, knifing through the water toward his roommate's dog in the surf.

"I was sure it was a shark," McDowell said, "and Steve's dog was out there. It all happened so fast I didn't have much time to think about it."

McDowell and his roommate, Steve Bailey, were living on Sullivan's Island, South Carolina, a small island near the entrance to Charleston Harbor. They had brought their dogs for a run along the beach when McDowell first saw the fin.

"When I got to the water, I saw it a second time and knew it wasn't a shark. I was curious and kept walking out deeper and deeper. When I got into chest-high water, the fish swam right by me, kind of slow. That's when I saw the bill and got excited. I figured it was a sailfish, so I just reached out and grabbed the fish by the tail."

As McDowell's fingers locked on to the base of the fish's tail, the startled creature lunged forward, pulling McDowell beneath the water. McDowell struggled to regain his balance, fighting to keep

Hayden McDowell (left), Steve Bailey, and Bailey's dog, Chappy, with a 38-pound longbill spearfish McDowell caught barehanded from the surf off Sullivan's Island, South Carolina

hold of the fish. He got a foothold in the sand and stood up, pulling the tail out of the water.

"I knew as long as I kept its tail above water, I could control it. I had to walk backward and almost lost the fish once when the water rose above my chest, but I held on, and when I hit the beach I was running.

"Steve came over and helped me drag the fish up on the sand. That's when I started jumping up and down. I kept yelling, 'It's a marlin! It's a marlin!'"

McDowell and Bailey took the billfish by pickup truck to the neighboring Isle of Palms, where it was weighed and recorded by a representative of the local Game and Fish Department. The representative took measurements and tissue samples, and two days later announced a surprising discovery.

The samples identified the fish, not as a small white marlin, as they first thought, but as a healthy female longbill spearfish. It was a fish that had never before been caught in South Carolina waters. The longbill spearfish weighed 38 pounds and measured 7 feet 2 inches.

One year later, a second longbill spearfish was caught off South Carolina, this time on rod and reel by angler Harry Johnson, confirming McDowell's claim to the discovery of a new species of game fish inhabiting the waters of South Carolina.

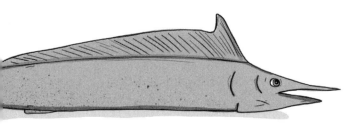

FATHER-SON PIKE VICTORY

Twelve-year-old Joe Miller sat on the grassy bank, watching his fishing bobber move with the breeze. It was mid-afternoon, and he was fishing with his dad and younger brother on Coeur d'Alene Lake near Post Falls, Idaho. A dead smelt dangled from the hook beneath the bobber, and young Joe hoped a hungry pike would swim by and gobble it up.

Joe had caught many small pike over the years, and he knew what to look for: slow movement as the pike gently mouths the bait and moves away. At 5:00 in the afternoon, he noticed his bobber drift off, then stop, then drift off again.

"I grabbed the fishing rod and yanked back hard," Joe said. "The response was deadweight. It was so heavy, I thought maybe I was snagged on an old boot or something, but then he took off for the middle of the lake."

The fish stayed out deep, refusing to budge. Joe hauled back against the weight. It was a standoff until finally, the line began to come in inches at a time. Joe's dad reminded him to be patient and not to tighten the drag too much. It was the biggest fish Joe had ever hooked and any misstep could be a disaster.

"I had forgotten our net," Joe said. "So finally when the fish came into the shallow water, my dad waded in and grabbed it by the head. Pike have sharklike teeth so he had to be careful. He got it onto shore, and we were amazed by its size. My dad had never seen such a large pike and he thought it might be a record."

The family hurried to the local tackle shop for a weight, but the first stop didn't have a certified scale. They drove to a grocery store called Y-J Foods and placed the fish on the scales.

"That pike weighed in at thirty-two pounds ten ounces. It was four feet long and measured two feet around the belly. It was my first really big pike."

Not only was it Joe's first big pike, but the fish set an Idaho state record.

"I can't believe I set a record, and I don't know if I'll ever catch a pike that big ever again. But I know that without my dad there to grab it and haul it from the water, I'd never have landed it."

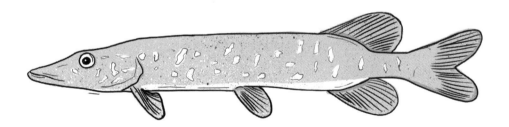

WRESTLING A 1,600-POUND HAMMERHEAD SHARK

CLASSIC

C aptain Jim Lewis was in the Bahama Islands enjoying a one-day break between fishing tournaments with his wife, Holly, and friends Rolando Encinosa and Andy Gill. It was early morning and their destination was Great Harbour Cay, a snorkelers' paradise 50 miles to the north of Chub Cay.

They had been traveling only 20 minutes when Lewis spotted what looked like the tail section of a small plane rising 2 to 3 feet above the water. Veering in for a closer look, they saw the mysterious tail section move and disappear beneath the water. Encinosa throttled the boat to full speed as Lewis ran to the bow and peered down into the clear water.

Fifteen feet below, swimming along the bottom of a narrow channel, was a huge hammerhead shark.

"Toss me a mask," Lewis yelled. "I'm going in!"

An experienced open-water diver, Lewis was confident that the swift current flowing through the narrow channel would confine the shark's movements. He slipped on the mask, clutched a short Hawaiian sling, and plunged into the water.

"The shark was enormous," Lewis said afterward, "and he knew

I was there. He would turn his head and roll back his eyes to look at me."

As his confidence mounted, Lewis dove deeper to study the shark. During one of his descents, he counted 19 remoras clinging to the shark's body and noticed several half-moon gaff scars along its side and back. The hammerhead was an old shark that had felt the sting of a hook many times before.

Lewis desperately wanted to hook the shark, but all his fishing gear was in Chub Cay. Only snorkel equipment was

Jim Lewis and his 1,600-pound hammerhead shark

readily available. And the Hawaiian sling, a three-prong hand spear propelled by a wristband.

"I knew my only chance was a shot in the gills," Lewis said. "The range of the sling was only five or six feet, so I had to get close. Still, I didn't know if it would be enough to stop the shark."

Lewis took a deep breath and kicked downward. His heart raced as he cocked the rubber band. He swam as close as he dared and fired. It was a perfect shot. The shark lunged toward Lewis, but it was weakened from the shot, and the strong current allowed Lewis time to reach the surface easily.

He climbed onto the boat and hurried to the bow. But the shark was swimming faster than before, blood streaming from its gills.

"What are you going to do now, Tarzan?" Encinosa joked.

Lewis didn't answer. The channel was getting deeper and would soon empty into open sea. He uncleated the grapple anchor and its 30 feet of chain, and yelled for Encinosa to drive ahead of the shark.

"It was all we had that resembled a hook," Lewis explained. "Roland drove ahead of the shark, and I threw out the anchor and let it sink to the bottom. When the shark swam by, I tried to snag him with it."

But to snag a shark with an anchor proved nearly impossible. Holly counted the attempts. On the 36th try, the shark jerked its head sideways and lunged at the anchor. Lewis pulled back, and miraculously the anchor slipped into the shark's wounded gill.

Lewis held the chain and Encinosa put the engines into neutral. The shark fought valiantly, towing the boat along the channel. But eventually the wounded shark tired and Lewis was able to haul it to the boat. Holly and Gill rushed to lasso the shark's huge tail.

Suddenly the hammerhead came to life, spinning dangerously alongside the boat. The powerful tail spun like a propeller, slapping Gill back across the deck and into the console, where he lay stunned on the floor.

"It was a crucial moment," Lewis said. "The shark was alive and we didn't have a gun on board, so we had to ground him."

They pulled the shark into the shallow water near one of the flats and waited. When he could approach safely, Lewis loosened the tail rope and wrapped it around the shark's head for the trip back to Chub Cay.

FISH FACT

Giant, sharp-toothed, 8-foot-long sand worms lurk beneath the beaches of Eastern Australia. Anglers drag raw meat over the sand to raise the worms, and then they snatch them by the neck and use them as bait for big surf bream and whiting.

At 3:00 in the afternoon, the small boat pulled up to the crowded dock. Onlookers watched as the shark was slowly raised from the largest scale in Chub Cay. But before the shark was fully aloft, the scale, reading 1,100 pounds, jammed and broke.

Fortunately, members of a University of Miami marine research team visiting Chub Cay were in the crowd. The marine biologists asked to take samples from the shark and offered to weigh it scientifically. Lewis gladly accepted the offer.

The shark was a great hammerhead that measured 15 feet 6 inches and had a girth of 10 feet 3 inches. It weighed an incredible 1,475 pounds. The team from Miami also examined the catch from head to tail. In the roof of the shark's mouth they counted 19 stingray barbs, while in its bulging belly they found a 110-pound lemon shark. The lemon shark was freshly eaten, sliced cleanly in half, and when added to the shark's weight pushed the final tally to nearly 1,600 pounds—more than 600 pounds over the current all-tackle world record.

THE GIRL WITH THE GOLDEN LURE

During her first big game fishing trip, Heidi Mason landed a 53-pound sailfish off the coast of Florida. She was 7 years old. At age 11, she caught a 308-pound hammerhead shark, and during that same year she released more than 25 sailfish, 11 of which were caught on 8-pound-test fishing line. She's also won or placed in almost every category of catch-and-release in Florida's largest fishing tournament, the annual MET (Metropolitan South Florida), including Top Angler 5 out of her first 6 years as a competitor.

At age 13, Mason was awarded Junior Master Angler in the tournament, and in the process landed her second world-record fish.

"Toward the end of the MET," Mason said, "Captain John Dudas took me and my father out to try to catch a winning fish. We decided to target amberjack, which, if I could catch and release enough of them, would give me the category for most releases."

Captain Dudas took Mason and her father to a wreck off Biscayne Bay. The fishing was good from the start, and the amberjack stayed hungry all day. Mason, who wanted to quickly release as many amberjack as she could, was using heavy tackle, including 80-pound-test line, to help combat the strong currents. Toward the end of the day, she decided to change gear and dropped to light tackle—her standard 8-pound test.

"We had been catching amberjack all day," she said, "so when the big one hit I was surprised by its strength. The fish was headed straight for the wreck and I didn't think I could stop it, but Captain Dudas was already moving the boat to help me as I pulled as hard as I could to turn the fish."

The tandem effort worked, and soon the battle became a test of endurance. Mason worked the fish halfway to the boat before the brute swam toward the sea floor, stripping away the line again and again. An hour passed before the fish finally tired. As it surfaced, Mason saw that instead of an amberjack, she was fighting an enormous African pompano. The fish was so large, she knew if she landed it, she would win first place in the tournament. Moments later, the fish was brought aboard to jubilation at her anticipated tournament win.

"It wasn't until the next day," Mason said, "that I realized the fish was a world record. I'd been looking at the record book, and I saw that my fish weighed thirty-four pounds more than the record. Luckily, we had weighed the pompano on a certified scale and had taken lots of photos for the MET Tournament."

The record pompano also qualified Mason for the Offshore Grand Champion Award for the 3rd year in a row. Then, just 2 years later, Mason became the youngest angler in MET history to win the acclaimed Master Angler Award. The feat is even more impressive, because Mason was competing against 20,000 entries, representing more than 40 states and 12 foreign countries.

Mason would go on to win more and more tournaments. She landed her third world record, a 463-pound hammerhead shark, on stand-up gear. Her fourth world record was a 66-pound cobia caught on 8-pound-test line off Miami, Florida. That battle lasted 3½ hours.

"When Heidi was a baby," her mother explained, "we had a huge mount of a hammerhead shark on the wall next to her changing table. Every time we changed her, she stared up at that shark. She was destined to catch big fish."

TRIPLE PLAY

It was late on a Friday afternoon when Billy Joe Hall headed out for reconnaissance at Lake Chickamauga just outside Dayton, Tennessee. He was looking for largemouth bass. There was a catch-and-release bass fishing tournament starting the next morning and he was doing research.

"We checked the sandbars," Hall said, "and spotted lots of little bass. So that was where we planned to start fishing in the morning."

Early Saturday morning, Hall arrived at his sandbar and started fishing the slate-colored shallows. The sky was clear, and the rising sun soon skipped coins of light off the mirrored surface. Cast after cast, however, resulted in nothing but empty water. Then, off in the distance, he spotted a large shad free-jump, soar through the air, and land on the bank. Hall reeled in his DD22 crank bait and let it fly.

"I'd seen a wake behind that shad," Hall explained, "so I knew a fish had been chasing it. I had cranked my lure eight or ten times when a bass loaded on and ran for a bit. And then it just bogged down like the line had wrapped a log or something."

Hall worked the mysterious weight back to the boat, and he noticed a large shadow appear beneath his lure. He would soon discover that it was a school of bass following his mysterious catch.

"The water was clear, and as I reeled a little more, we saw a grouping of three bass hooked to my lure. It was unbelievable! Every hook had a big bass on it. I told my buddy to try and net at least two of them."

His buddy did better than that. All three bass were boated and each weighed an impressive 5 to 6 pounds.

"Those other bass that followed my three fish to the boat had hung around, so as my buddy loaded the fish into the live well, I grabbed another rod and cast a spinner bait and got another one. The tournament limit was eight fish, and so we kept fishing and landed a total of seven fish there. It was some of the best fishing you could imagine. Eventually the bite slowed, so we moved on and caught our eighth at another spot. By the time we made it to the scales, two of the fish had died and we were penalized a pound for each. Still, we won the tournament by a long shot, with forty-six-and-a-half pounds of bass."

Hall, who not long after was diagnosed with cancer, remembers that day fondly.

"I beat the odds that day," he said, "and then, with the Good Lord looking over me, I beat the odds again."

While it may have been divine intervention that led to Hall's recovery, there can be no doubt that landing three 6-pound large-mouth bass on a single lure was a fishing miracle.

HER WEIGHT IN BASS

Thirteen-year-old Terrie Allen fished with her dad often, usually on the Santa Monica Pier or on one of the weekend half-day boats heading out of San Pedro, California. Barracuda and calico bass were their usual targets, and over the years they had caught too many to count.

"On this day," Terrie recalled, "my dad and I were out at Catalina Island, hoping for some big calicos. The bass were plentiful, and the bait wells were just brimming with live anchovies. I found a fat lively one and pinned it on the hook and dropped it over the rail."

Terrie knew the big bass took their time, and so she waited for what seemed like an eternity. Worried that her bait was stuck in seaweed or hidden beneath a rocky ledge, she reached for the reel, and the rod doubled over and nearly pulled her overboard.

"I knew the fish was headed for the rocks, so I hauled back as hard as I could to try to stop it. Somehow it worked and the fish slowed. I tightened the drag and held on for thirty minutes of give and take, hardly moving the fish at all."

Terrie made progress, inches at a time. Her arms ached as the fish swung for the seafloor. She leaned back and again tightened the drag, worried that the line would break.

"It was the biggest fish I'd ever fought. I thought for sure it would win the fight and spit the hook or the line would break. I was the youngest person on the boat and the only girl. I didn't want to lose that fish."

Finally, the fish rose to within gaffing distance. The deckhand quickly plunged a gaff into the water and hauled aboard the biggest fish of the year. It wasn't a calico or a barracuda, it was a giant sea bass.

The captain came down from the bridge and congratulated his young angler on her catch, and told her he'd notified the outdoor editor of the local paper. He also told her she'd won the daily jackpot for the biggest fish caught on the boat, an especially satisfying win because all the other anglers on board that day were adults.

Back at the dock, the fish weighed in at 103 pounds. The reporter from the Los Angeles *Examiner* interviewed Terrie, and the story ran all across the state. The headline read, "Girl—105 Pounds— Bags 103-Pound Sea Bass."

Terrie not only won the jackpot, but the tackle manufacturer that outfitted the boat sent her a custom-made rod and reel with her name engraved on the shaft.

"The best part," Terrie, now an adult, said, "was sharing the experience with my dad. He was so proud of me. He was the reason I fished, and he's the reason I still fish to this day."

WORLD'S LARGEST FRESHWATER FISH

It was a Saturday morning, approaching noon, when Joey Pallotta and a friend arrived at the docks in Benicia, California. They bought a scoop of grass shrimp at the local bait shop and boarded Joey's boat, steering west through Carquinez Strait toward San Francisco Bay.

"The wind was really blowing on the bay," Pallotta said, "so we turned back into the strait. On our way back, I saw a fish jump. The water was pretty deep there and I liked the area, so we anchored down and rigged the shrimp."

Ten minutes passed without any luck. Pallotta's eyes constantly skimmed the water's surface, his view never leaving the rod. As a slight breeze rocked the boat, the rod tip began to bounce gently. It was the pump of a sturgeon strike. Pallotta carefully lifted the rod from the holder and waited.

"He was a suicide fish," Pallotta said. "When I picked up the rod, I expected to wait for the usual third or fourth pump, but this fish immediately pulled straight down."

Pallotta reined back on the rod, digging the hooks deeply into the fish's leathery mouth. The fish hovered near the bottom, then surged upward, splitting the surface scarcely 50 yards away. It thrashed on the surface and then plunged back to the muddy bottom. Palotta worried as the line poured from the spool. "The tide was pulling the fish down the strait and into the bay. We were in trouble, so we cut the anchor rope and went out with him. He was a strong fish, and for the first two hours I never gained any line."

Eventually, the tide shifted and the sturgeon returned to the strait. Pallotta had fought many sturgeons before, but none as powerful as this.

"A good friend of mine, Tom Galakeler, was fishing close by," Pallotta said. "His boat was bigger, and he agreed to come help me out."

Other boats drifted nearby, the fishermen hoping to see the monster sturgeon. Pallotta's line began to rise. The fish rushed the surface and jumped a second time. It was enormous.

"After he jumped," Pallotta said, "he really began to fight. He took multiple runs up and down and around the boat. We pulled him toward the shallows and he pulled us toward the bay. Nobody seemed to be winning."

FISH FACT
Sea stars, also known as starfish, eat clams by prying open their shells and then extending their bellies from their mouths into the open shell to digest the clam.

Pallotta's reel began to malfunction. It continued to overheat, forcing him to pour cool water over the spool. Galakeler, meanwhile, did what he could, watching the line and keeping the boat in neutral for the fish to tow.

The sturgeon came to the surface 13 times without confronting the gaff.

Joey Pallotta with his 468-pound world-record sturgeon

Then, at 8:15 in the evening, the fish surfaced for the 14th and final time.

"He fought hard at the gaff," Pallotta said, "but we held tight. When he stopped splashing, we tied him to the stern. The boat's beam was twelve feet, and the sturgeon stretched easily from one end to the other."

The record sturgeon was still alive, and the dock was only 5 minutes away. When he arrived, Pallotta ran to a telephone and called the Steinhart Aquarium. He wanted to save the fish if he could. But the biologist at the Aquarium wasn't interested. Pallotta was forced to make a difficult decision.

"Part of me wanted to let him go. I'd fished most of my life, and I cared a lot about these fish. I guess I finally decided that I deserved the record, and that I could make this fish live forever."

Pallotta's next call was to the local Game and Fish Department. His record catch needed an accurate weight from a registered scale, but the scale at Benicia measured only to 300 pounds—not enough. Next, Pallotta and Galakeler loaded the fish into a truck, and started toward a certified truck scale in Fairfield, 45 minutes away. When they arrived, it was midnight and the scales were closed.

They drove to the C&H Sugar Refinery in Crockett, a half-hour drive farther inland. But state health regulations barred weighing fish on their scales.

Frustrated, tired, and out of ideas, the two fishermen drove to a friend's house nearby.

"My buddy's wife," Pallotta explained, "knew someone at the Sante Fe Railroad Station. It was two thirty in the morning by the time she called him, but he agreed to weigh the fish."

After hours of drying in the sultry night air, the fish was finally properly weighed and registered an impressive 468 pounds. Pallotta and Galakeler placed the fish in a walk-in freezer and waited for daylight.

The next morning the media were notified, and reporters and photographers arrived in droves to meet the local angler responsible for the world's largest freshwater catch.

"We hung the fish on the local scale," Pallotta said, "but it broke. Then everything went wild. Cameras were flashing and everybody was asking me questions. It was really something."

The fish was filleted and the skin was stretched and dried for mounting. A mold was made and the first cast hung proudly above Pallotta's fireplace. A huge poster-size photograph was later hung on his living room wall and another in the local bait shop.

Since then, maximum size limits have been set for sturgeon fishing, assuring Pallotta the top spot in the record books. And unless the restrictions change, his fish will, as Pallotta wished, live forever.

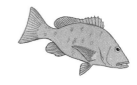

SNAGGED BY A DOG-TOOTHED SNAPPER

When they weren't spearfishing from a rubber dinghy off Baja California, Mexico, 12-year-old Tim Vermilya and his younger brother, David, spent their time deep-sea fishing.

"We used to go camping in Mexico each year," Tim said. "We'd camp on a beach with a big bay and lots of rocks. The spearfishing was always great, and nearby was always a fish camp, where we could charter a *panga* and go fishing."

Tim's dad, once a commercial fishing captain, had started both sons fishing at a young age. By the age of 10, Tim had caught his first billfish—a 130-pound sailfish—and he caught it in Mexico from a *panga*.

It was during one of the family's annual Baja camping trips that Tim found himself near Las Arenas, 60 miles south of La Paz. The expansive beach was prime territory for big game fishing. Marlin, yellowtail, wahoo, and all the other exotics regularly cruised these pristine shores.

"We had seen a lot of fish while spearfishing," Tim said. "Especially big yellowtail. So one morning my dad hired a *panga* to take us out fishing. As soon as we got to the deep water, we started jigging for the big yellows. Almost immediately, I hooked a fish and it took a lot of line fast. It was headed for the rocks, but I couldn't stop it. Our captain gunned the engine and took off for deeper water to try to turn it. I was using forty-pound-test line and was sure it would break."

But the fishing line held and the fish was successfully pulled into the deep water and away from the safety of the rocks. Tim leaned back against the weight and wondered if the fish had somehow anchored itself to the bottom. His arms burned and his back ached. Slowly the fish inched back toward the rocks, and stubbornly Tim brought it back to the deep water.

Thirty minutes passed before the line began to give slightly. Tim arched his back and gained a bit of line. The captain shouted encouragements and the deckhand readied the gaff. Tim pulled with all the strength he had left. A shadow emerged and the air erupted in excited Spanish as the deckhand cried out *"Pargo grande!"* and freed a second gaff from the gunwale.

FISH FACT

Lobster blood is colorless until exposed to air. Then, because of its copper content, the blood turns blue, not red. Boiling lobsters live keeps the blood from exposure.

"When we saw what it was, we couldn't believe it—a huge dog snapper, a fish that doesn't hit a jig. They usually take bait, and then they race into the rocks and break off the line. At this point it was getting late, so the captain took us back to our campsite. On the way in he

Twelve-year-old Tim Vermilya with one of the largest dog-toothed snappers, known locally as pargo, ever caught

said it was the biggest *pargo* he had ever seen. But there were no scales on the beach so all we took were photographs. Then I gave the fish to the captain, who filleted it and sold it. When we got home and showed the pictures, people told us it was probably a world record on forty-pound line."

Tim and his family continue to fish Baja, and they have yet to catch or hear of a larger *pargo* coaxed from the rocks of Baja California's Sea of Cortez.

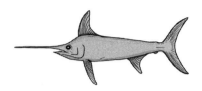

SWORD FROM THE SURF

Marco Ehrenberg and his friend Victor Gutierrez were cruising in a Jeep along Baja California's La Paz *Malecón*, a beautiful bayside walkway famous for its sunsets. It was mid-afternoon and locals and tourists were milling about enjoying the bay breeze.

"I saw splashes near shore," Marco explained, "and I thought it was a dolphin. Then I thought it was a shark. I told Victor to stop the car."

Marco leaped from the passenger seat and raced into the water. He waded into the calm shallow bay and swam out to grab the fish by the tail.

"That's when I thought maybe I had made a mistake."

The fish turned and slashed its bill across his knee. Swordfish! Marco fell back, still holding the tail, while the momentum pushed the two toward shore.

"I probably should have let go, but I was young and didn't know how dangerous this was. I had a big fish by the tail and it was going crazy and I just held on."

A nearby local fisherman saw Marco struggling with the fish and tossed him a fish bat with a bent nail that served as a make-shift gaff. Marco lunged with the weapon, but the fish was too big.

"Everything was happening so fast, and I was very lucky. The swordfish was disoriented and we were moving into the shallow rocks. The people on the *Malecón* were cheering me on. I had hold of the fish and wanted to land it, so I used a rock to subdue it, and then Victor helped me haul it up the beach."

The swordfish was carried to the Jeep and placed into the backseat, where it was so long that both its tail and sword stuck out on the sides.

"My knee was hurting, but I didn't care. I'd caught a hundred-twenty-pound swordfish with my bare hands. My friend's mom lived nearby, so we took the swordfish to her house and she made enough swordfish meatballs to feed family and friends for weeks. They were the best meatballs I've ever eaten in my life."

Before the fish was cleaned, a local reporter heard about the story and raced out for photos and an interview. He titled his story "Two Men Risk Their Lives for a Swordfish." As Marco recalls, "I guess in a way we did. My knee was sore for a long time, and looking back, I now know how dangerous a swordfish bill can be, but at the time I didn't even think about it. We were lucky. Everything went right that day: the fish pushed me toward shore instead of back out into the deeper water, the fisherman who came along with the homemade gaff, and the loose rocks I could use to end the fight. I was lucky that fish didn't hurt me a lot worse."

FISHING TEEN AND MIGHTY MARLIN

Captain Momi Bean, a third-generation Hawaiian, was destined to become a professional fisherman. His father and grandfather were both fishermen, and as far back as Momi can remember, he was on the sea, helping his father catch tuna for the local markets. As a young man, he worked as a deckhand for a legendary local captain, Bobby Brown, and learned the skills to become a big-game captain. But of all his catches, the one that stands out the most is the fish he caught as a 13-year-old, fishing with his younger cousin, from his dad's small outboard boat.

Momi and his cousin were 18 miles off the big island of Hawaii when they stopped at a buoy and landed a 9-pound aku, also known as a skipjack tuna, for bait. Momi quickly rigged the tuna and sent it down on 130-pound-test fishing line. Then they slowly circled the buoy.

"Suddenly, my fishing rod buckled," Momi said. "The reel spun with a loud whir and was moving way too fast and was way too hot to touch. I left it in the holder and turned the boat and chased the fish. I knew it wasn't a big tuna because it stayed on the surface. Then it jumped and I could see that it was a big marlin. The drag was set tight so I put the boat into neutral and let it pull us to try to tire it out."

The rod holder was built to rotate with the boat, so as the marlin changed directions, the boat followed without breaking the fishing rod. Finally, the marlin slowed, and Momi cranked in line, leaving the fishing rod in its holder. For 30 minutes, he fought the big fish, and then it surged off into the distance once again. Momi ran to the boat controls and followed. An hour and a half later, the marlin finally tired.

"It surfaced with the leader wrapped around its body, so when I pulled, it spun upside down. It was tired, but it was still fighting. At one point it went under the boat and I couldn't hang on to the leader. As it went from port to starboard, I dropped the leader and grabbed the stick gaff. Somehow I got the gaff in, and then grabbed a smaller hand gaff and got that in it, too. I roped two half-hitches around its bill and tied the rope to the cleat, but just as I finished, the stick gaff splashed into the water and floated away. Luckily, I had the marlin's head above water so I knew it couldn't go anywhere."

FISH FACT
The flathead gudgeon can float upside down in debris before pouncing on its unsuspecting victims.

Momi worked fast, grabbing a flying gaff and securing the marlin to the side of the small skiff. He tied its head to the bow and its tail to the stern. It was an enormous marlin, nearly the entire length of the boat. It took 3½ hours to tow the catch back to Kona. Moni had no radio on board, but a nearby boat had witnessed the incredible catch and radioed the information to a local radio station for its daily fish report. The station broadcaster contacted Momi's family with the news.

"My family arrived at the pier and watched as I entered the harbor. The boat tilted to one side and was moving slowly because of the extra weight."

A large group of onlookers had also amassed to watch the startling catch hoisted to the scales. The weighmaster climbed the scale ladder and announced "925 pounds!" to the cheering crowd. The marlin measured 17 feet in length and was the largest fish ever caught by a 13-year-old in Hawaii.

"Looking back," Captain Bean said, "I realize how lucky I was that everything went right. I'll never forget that day. It was one of the best days of my life."

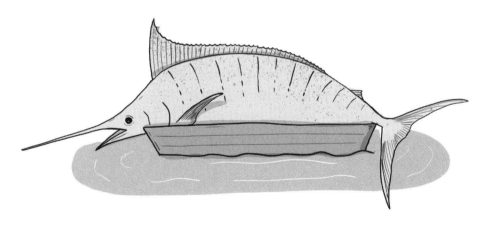

FEET ON THE SHORE, MARLIN ON THE LINE

Vicki Lear stared across the canvas of deep water as she fished from the rocks of Jervis Bay, New South Wales, Australia. It was January 5, 1999, and she was the only woman angler on the cliff. That wasn't unusual. In fact, since she started fishing the prolific bay back in 1992, she'd yet to see another female angler.

"In my twenty-odd years of fishing," Lear said, "I have seen the numbers of women grow in the sport but at a very slow pace. From one to two ladies in a tournament, now it's often four or more, and the same goes for fishing club attendance."

Lear is certainly doing her part as well. Sponsored by many of the biggest names in fishing gear, Lear regularly competes in tournaments, writes articles for fishing magazines, and is a regular contributor to the website lureandfly.com. She's also done what no other female angler has done before. She broke a decades-old women's tournament record for striped marlin on 8-kilogram-test line (17-pound test) by landing an 81-kilo (179-pound) striped marlin to win the Port Stephens New South Wales Tournament. She's also the only woman to land a black marlin from shore using stand-up gear and 10-kilogram-test line (22-pound test).

"It's an area known as the Tubes," she explained, "named after

Vicki Lear on shore. Marlin on the line.

an old torpedo tube from the war days. It's a popular fishing spot because it's accessible through a bush track that's been cut from the parking lot."

Popular, but not your typical shoreline for surf fishing. The trek from the parking lot winds through groves of red bloodwood trees and dense shrubs and sedges. Sandstone plateaus descend to rocky precipices that are severe in places and where the water drops into deep powerful currents. The fishing, however, can be spectacular. Many large pelagic species migrate into the deepwater bay, everything from kingfish to yellowfin tuna and black marlin. And when the bite is hot, the crowds can make the already treacherous fishing chaotic with tangles, snags, and broken fishing lines.

"Usually there are a dozen or so people fishing," Lear said, "but if the fishing is good, there can be up to forty lines in the water."

To avoid crossing lines and tangled gear, anglers have devised an unwritten system similar to surfers lining up for a swell. At each prime location, one angler deploys his bait beneath a balloon that serves as a bobberlike sail, taking the bait far beyond casting distance with the wind and current. The idea is to get the drifting bait past the drop-off. As the drift heads out, the next angler will deploy their live bait, and so on. If there is difficulty with the bait not drifting in the right location, a tangle with another angler, or it is suspected the bait is not swimming correctly, the angler will reel in and move to the back of the lineup.

"It works pretty well," Lear said. "The day I caught my marlin, I'd been to the back of the line a couple of times."

When her turn came around again, Lear grabbed a mackerel from the inflatable kid's swimming pool she'd filled by bucketing water from the shore. The pool was fitted with an aerator to keep the bait lively, one of which she pinned to a 7-ought hook. She was using a big game

Lear's marlin. Note the balloon visible above the tail.

rod, Shimano Beastmaster reel, and a length of 80-pound leader. She rigged a balloon to the swivel and sent the contraption floating with the wind and current.

"You hope the bait gets out to where the fish are," she said, "and then you hope the marlin doesn't take you too far out or into Eddy's Rock."

The week before, Lear had lost an estimated 100-pound marlin to an anchor line far out in the bay when the fish took too much line in a blistering first run. This time, however, Lear's marlin avoided the boats fishing the outer bay and instead headed straight for Eddy's Rock.

She hooked a marlin quickly, but just as fast, Lear tells, "It started greyhounding toward the rock, which has broken off countless fish over the years, so I loosened the drag to try to turn it without getting a backlash on the reel."

The strategy worked, and for the next 20 minutes, Lear carefully worked the marlin to the rock shore. As the fish closed in, other anglers worked their way to the lowest ledge of rock and readied the gaff.

"I could tell it was small, and normally I wouldn't take a small marlin, but this was my first and only marlin caught from the rocks, and the fish was wiped out. That's another thing about fishing the rocks at Jervis Bay. Without a boat backing down on the fish, it's a much longer fight and the marlin come in nearly dead. We had one guy go into the water with a marlin to try to revive it. He swam that fish out into the currents for an hour, but it didn't work."

Lear's fish was hauled back to her car and taken to the Currarong Bowling Club, where the fish weighed in at 21 kilograms (46 pounds). She had it mounted, and today it hangs proudly from a wall in her home.

"My husband caught a marlin from the rocks on a different trip, and that one weighed sixty-eight kilos [one hundred fifty pounds]. But we haven't been back since. It was something I always wanted to do, and once I did it, I moved on to other kinds of fishing."

And most likely more records and tournament wins for this talented and prolific angler.

For more photos and a video of Vicki's marlin catch, visit lureandfly.com.

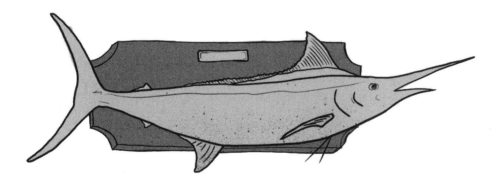

RECORD OF STEEL

On a typical summer day off Bell Island, Alaska, 8-year-old David White and his family were fishing from an inflatable dinghy at 6:00 in the evening. The fishing had been slow, so White ignored his dad's instructions and dropped his bait to the bottom, where it kept snagging on rocks.

"My dad had already freed three or four of my snags," White said, "and he was getting frustrated. He warned me that if it happened again, I'd be in trouble. Even though I was scared, I dropped my bait down deep again."

Suddenly, White's rod slumped forward again, moving slowly, just as it had on the previous snags. "I started letting line out so I wouldn't get in trouble. My dad saw me and his face got red. He was really mad. I told him I thought I had a fish, but he could see how slow the line was moving. As he stopped the boat, my line shot across the water. I shouted that I had something. My brothers reeled in their lines, and my dad killed the engine. Everyone watched as the fish raced at least a hundred yards out to sea and then started jumping."

The fish was so far away that it looked small. It also fought just like the salmon they had caught earlier on the trip. Only this fish was stronger. Each time White reeled in line, the fish took it away.

"When it was about halfway to the boat, it jumped again and we saw how big it was. We couldn't believe it!"

It was the largest fish any of them had ever hooked. It charged deep. It surfaced and sulked, then sounded again. It circled the boat in great bursts of speed. Then, without warning, the line slackened. White reeled frantically, tears welling in his young eyes.

"I felt the line go dead and thought for sure the fish was gone. I reeled as fast as I could

Eight-year-old David White with his record steelhead

and saw this shadow in the water that looked like a submarine. It was huge, and it surfaced about ten feet from the boat. Then it slowly drifted away and my line followed it. I was still hooked up!"

White pulled with all of his remaining strength. His dad readied the net and dipped it gently into the water. White carefully guided his line toward the net.

"We learned later that the fish couldn't see the net. It had so

FISH FACT
Fossils unearthed in China have dated fishlike creatures to 530 million years old.

many scars on its face and it had lost an eye. It was old, which is probably why we got it on the first try. But it definitely had more fight left, because when it hit the net, it went nuts. Water was flying everywhere."

White's dad hauled the catch aboard, where it flopped dangerously around the boat. White and his brother dived on top of it, pinning it with their arms and legs. It was now 10:00 in the evening. The scales were still open, and the fish was hoisted into the air. It weighed in at 42 pounds 2 ounces. The weighmaster placed it in the freezer, where it was flash frozen. Weeks later, it was sent to a taxidermist in Seattle, Washington. While curing the skin, the taxidermist noticed that the pattern resembled a steelhead rather than a salmon as first suspected. The fish was quickly sent to the University of Washington, where the founder of the fisheries department, Dr. Lauren Donaldson, confirmed the taxidermist's suspicions. White's parents took the finding and submitted the catch to the International Game Fish Association, where the fish was qualified as a world record. It was the largest steelhead ever caught on rod and reel.

"I was just a little kid," White recalled. "I didn't care what kind of fish it was, but when they told me it was a world record, I was the happiest kid around."

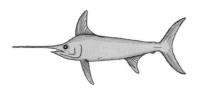

SWORDFISH TUG-OF-WAR

Just the mention of swordfish is enough to incite passion in the hearts of fishermen. Famed for their unyielding strength and defiance of the hook, the broadbill has pushed many anglers toward obsession and reduced others to states of delirium.

But the years have not been kind to the swordfish. Their prized flanks bring a high price at market, and competition for these golden billfish is fierce. Don and Millie Allison know firsthand just how fierce that can be.

They were in southern California in the early 1970s aboard the *Hoaloha*, their 42-foot custom Hatteras. Two experienced anglers out for an enjoyable day of fishing, they had the good fortune of coming upon a large swordfish sunning its back in the waters off Santa Barbara Island. The broadbill, an old warrior missing the tip of its dorsal fin, was slowly cruising south across the afternoon chop.

"Millie took the controls," Don recalled, "while I went down and rigged a fresh mackerel. She eased up close, and I dropped the bait into the water. Minutes later we had the hookup."

The two anglers were prepared for the expected battle, and an hour and a half later the fish finally surfaced. It was a magnificent swordfish, big and strong and thick across the shoulders. Don cranked the reel evenly, working the rod with care. Millie patiently worked the boat, as she had many times before.

The swordfish was less than two boat-lengths away, when suddenly, from abeam the boat, came a large commercial vessel, full speed ahead, the plank off its bow bearing down on their catch. It was the *Santa Lucia*, a local commercial harpooning boat intent on the Allisons' swordfish.

"Don't hit that fish!" Millie screamed. "He's on our line!" But the man on the plank ignored her pleas, reared back, and thrust a deadly harpoon into the hooked fish. Coils of thick yellow nylon rope and brightly colored floats followed.

"We've just stuck a rod-and-reel fish!" the captain of the *Santa Lucia* declared excitedly to a friend over the radio. "Whose is it?"

"Whoever has the heaviest gear," replied the friend.

Millie was irate. The swordfish had sounded, and while Don worked feverishly to retrieve it, she maneuvered the boat to keep their line away from the harpooner's coarse rope. Meanwhile, the *Santa Lucia* circled, waiting for the harpoon buoys to resurface.

Twenty more minutes passed before the wounded fish was again within gaffing range. Don seized the leader and gaffed the fish. He cut the harpooner's rope from the buoys and tied the fish to the stern. Millie turned and headed back to port.

Still circling nearby, the *Santa Lucia* called the Allisons on the radio.

"We got it in the head, didn't we?" they taunted.

The Allisons did not respond, and the *Santa Lucia* quickly faded from sight.

Many other boats had been tuned to the same radio frequency and had heard the confrontation. By the time the Allisons arrived back at the dock, the airwaves from San Diego to San Francisco were buzzing with the news. The swordfish was hoisted to the weighscale with the dart of the harpoon still lodged by its dorsal. The fish weighed 448 pounds—the largest catch of the year.

Elated by the catch, the Allisons did not file a complaint against the *Santa Lucia* or its crew. Their tarnished reputation, the result of all the publicity about the incident, would suffice.

The harpoon dart was saved, however, as a reminder of the year's most unusual catch.

PHOTO CREDITS

p. xii, courtesy of Patsy Morey; p. 2, courtesy of Eleanor M. L. Choy; p. 4, courtesy of Matt Watson; p. 8, courtesy of Glenda Rosenbalm; p. 26, courtesy of Cairns Game Fishing Club and Capt. George Bransford; p. 30, courtesy of Art Gardner and Dave Romeo; p. 34, courtesy of Dr. Hal Neibling; p. 40, courtesy of Gary Hansford; p. 43, courtesy of Calvin Nolan; p. 52, Burton McNeely/ Getty Images; p. 55, courtesy of Capt. Alan Card; p. 61, Picavet/ Getty Images; p. 67, dhogan172/fotolia; p. 73, Raul Touzon/Getty Images; p. 100, courtesy of Capt. Ed Murray; p. 102, courtesy of Blake Robinson; p. 107, Richard Clark/Getty Images; p. 110, Nikolai Sorokin/fotolia; p. 164, courtesy of Dick Rankin; p. 166, courtesy of Capt. Snooks Fuller; p. 170, courtesy of Adam Konrad and Sean Konrad; p. 173, courtesy of Terry Joyce; p. 178, courtesy of Captain Jim Lewis; p. 190, courtesy of Joey Pallotta; p. 195, courtesy of Tim Vermilya; pp. 202 and 203, courtesy of Vicki Lear; p. 207, courtesy of David White.